Items should be returned on or be~~~~~~~~~~~~~~~~~~~
shown below. Items not already re~~~~~~~~~~~~~~~~~
borrowers may be renewed in person, in writing or by
telephone. To renew, please quote the number on the
barcode label. To renew online a PIN is required.
This can be requested at your local library.
Renew online @ **www.dublincitypubliclibraries.ie**
Fines cha~~~~~~~~~~~~~~~~~~~~overdue items will include postage
incur~
be ~

Kenny's Choice

First published by Currach Press 2008
55A Spruce Avenue, Stillorgan Industrial Park, Blackrock, County Dublin
www.currach.ie
Reprinted in 2015
Cover design and inside photographs by Bluett
Origination by Currach Press
Printed by ScandBook
ISBN: 9781782188513

Kenny's Choice

101 Irish Books You *Must* Read

Des Kenny

CURRACH
PRESS

In Kate O'Brien's *Without My Cloak*, as Molly Considine is dressing for an important dinner party, Anthony, her husband, says to her, 'You must be the loveliest woman in Christendom this night…I've never looked on anyone so beautiful.'

Anthony Considine was wrong. My wife Anne is the most beautiful woman in Christendom

and

to her beauty
tto her steadfastness
to her absolute refusal to be anything else
but that which she is
I dedicate this book.

'There are no days more full in childhood than those days that are not lived at all, the days lost in a book.'

John McGahern

'Once you have a book, you are never bored.'

Maureen Kenny

'The book salesman should be honoured because he brings to our attention, as a rule, the very books we need most and neglect most.'

Confucius

Acknowledgements

Although my name appears on the title page of this book, many other people were an integral part of it. Central to it were my parents Maureen and Des Kenny, without whom it would never have happened.

I would like to pay tribute to my maternal grandmother, the only grandparent I ever knew, Jane Canning. Her brown bread and reading of the adventures of Count Curly Wee sustained me physically and mentally as I headed to college each morning. Also to my late sister-in-law Catherine whose wonderful lunches and warm encouragement kept me going through the long hot summer before my BA exam.

My siblings and their spouses were an essential part of the book and I would like to thank Thomas and Maureen, Jane and Billy, Gerry and Anne, Monica and Frank, and Conor and Geraldine.

Those who suffered most during the writing of this book were my wife Anne, to whom it is dedicated, our four wonderful children and their partners, Deirdre and Mark, Dessy and Pamela, Aisling and Joe, and Eimear our thespian. My nephew Tomás, who shares my office, also shared many of my more difficult moments and his suggestions were always helpful.

Our staff also had an essential role to play. To our first employee, the late Olive Smith, and to all those who have helped the wheel turn for nearly seventy years, I express my appreciation I would like to thank Elaine Murphy who patiently typed up my scrawls and Dean Kelly whose creative skills produced the photographs and jackets.

I thank Michael Brennan, that peerless publisher's representative, who caught the hopped ball and ran with it, my editor Jo O'Donoghue, who put her faith in the project and gently helped it come to life, and all those at Currach Press who have added their expertise to ensure the book came to fruition.

A book of this nature requires a basic reference work and here I acknowledge *The Oxford Companion to Irish Literature* edited by Robert Welch, a deep well of information from which I drank regularly.

I would like to thank others who helped in different ways.

- Norman Morgan, the Loughrea bibliophile who provided the first editions of Seamus O'Kelly's *The Weaver's Grave*
- Joe and Theresa Gleeson whose home in Ballyferriter provided a delightful haven in which the book went over the half-way line
- Sculptor John Coll whose bronzes adorn the entries for John Millington Synge, Samuel Beckett and Patrick Kavanagh
- Sculptor John Behan whose *Famine Ship* provides the illustration for Cecil Woodham Smith's *The Great Hunger*
- Mark Finegan, whose instinctive photo adorns the back cover
- Artist Pauline Bewick whose painting helps bring *The Midnight Court* to life
- Colin Smythe for permission to use the covers for *The Turf-cutter's Donkey*, *The Untilled Field* and *Traits and Stories of the Irish Peasantry*
- Mercier Press for permission to use the covers for *The Course of Irish History*, *The Tailor and Ansty* and *The Great O'Neill*

- Penguin for permission to use the covers for *Woodbrook* and *Puckoon*
- Collins Press for permission to use the covers for *The Hard Road to Klondike* and *The Last of the Name*
- Virago Press for permission to use the cover of *Never No More*
- New Island Press for permission to use the cover for *The Visitor*
- Wolfhound/Merlin Press for permission to use the cover for *The Ancient Books of Ireland* and *The Unfortunate Fursey*
- Irish Academic Press for permission to use the cover for *The Moynihan Brothers*
- The Salmon Press for permission to use the cover for *The White Page/An Bhileog Bhán*
- Appletree Press for permission to use the cover for *Hurrish*
- Arlen House for permission to use the cover for *Dhá Scéal/Two Stories*
- Poetry Ireland/Éigse Éireann for permission to use the cover for *Watching the River Flow*
- Brandon Press for permission to use the cover for *Michael Joe*
- Patrick MacManus who provided the photo of his father Francis MacManus
- Aileen Wall who provided the photo of her father Mervyn Wall
- Séamus Tomás O'Crohan who provided the photos that illustrate the entry for *An tOileánach*
- Cole Moreton who dug into his archives to provide the photograph of himself and his son Jake
- Joe O'Shaughnessy for his delightful photograph of

Mother dressing the Seamus Heaney window the day Heaney's Nobel Prize was announced

- Geoffrey Moorhouse who provided the photo for *Sun Dancing*
- Charlie Byrne and Vinny Murphy from Charlie Byrne's Bookshop who provided a number of out-of-print texts that had proven to be elusive

Mick Moloney of Setanta Communications was most generous with his advice in regard to the illustrations that were best suited to the project.

Outside my own family a number of people gave most helpful advice with the earlier drafts of the introduction. In this respect I would like to thank Galway classicist Professor Brian Arkins, Corkman and respected adviser Jim Hyland, the discerning bibliophiles Brian and Maureen McLaughlin, two of my French musketeers, Catherine Cheval and Marie Ploux, our American champions Tony and Lynn Hughes and our Dublin full-back Ronan Richmond of Argosy.

Tá mé fíor-bhuíoch freisin de Ger Fitz a léigh na sliochtaí as Gaeilge agus a thug cabhair agus comhairle den scoth dom.

I would like to thank all the writers who had the belief to write these books, the publishers who had the courage to publish them, the publishers' representatives who had the stamina to bring them to our attention and the customers who, over the last twenty years, have made and continue to make the ultimate act of faith in us.

Proofreading is not by any means my strongest suit and here I acknowledge the youthful eyes of Claire O'Shaughnessy. Finally, I would like to say a special thank you to Cormac 'Speedy' Burke, Gerry's right-hand man, who is also, sometimes, thankfully, mine.

Contents

Introduction

People thought them mad when on 29 November 1940 Des and Maureen Kenny opened the doors of their spanking new second-hand bookshop in High Street, Galway. Various stories have come down to us from that day, but perhaps the most telling was mother's recollection: 'I remember the day as being fairly quiet but at the end of it our hearts were full of hope and joy.'

Five years earlier, Maureen had left her native Mohill in County Leitrim to pursue a Commerce degree in University College Galway. As she walked to college on her first day and started up St Mary's Road, Des Kenny emerged from Raleigh Row and that – or at least so they always told us – was that. They were married in Mohill.

For us six children, our parents and the shop were synonymous. Although Father had to work elsewhere for twenty years to feed and clothe his growing family, he never really left the bookshop. We grew up in a household that was sustained by the twin pulses of books and love. Books were everywhere in our house in Kingshill, Salthill: on the stairs, under the stairs, over the stairs, in the bedrooms and bathroom. There was no wall space that hadn't been, at some stage, shelved and filled with books. Books were also put to practical use. Conor's cot was a drawer that had been emptied of a collection of scarce pamphlets relating to Irish history and it was propped up by four folio volumes of eighteenth-century theology.

Apart from Our Lady's Boy's Club, the Soroptomists and the Irish Water Safety Association, the sole topic of our parents' conversation was books. At the dinner table or during their nightly walks on the promenade, they talked about how such or such an author was shaping up and what titles they could offer their various customers. A vivid childhood memory is of father backing the car, laden with the contents of a library he had bought somewhere, down the little hill to the front door of our house of a winter's evening. After a hot bath, he would sit by the fire in the sitting room with an onion sandwich and a bottle of stout. Those of us who hadn't managed to make ourselves scarce unloaded the books.

Father would tell us that this library was going to make us rich beyond our wildest dreams, then would suddenly ask anxiously: 'Did you find it, did you find it?' He wanted to be sure that we hadn't missed the two or three items on which he had based the price paid for the whole library, knowing that Mother had a customer for them and hoping for a quick sale to cover the cheque he had written. Meanwhile, we were trying to sneak the books we found most interesting up to our rooms, in case she had a customer for *them*.

From early on, our parents sold paintings from the back of the shop. They had a strong belief that Irish artists were at least as good as their vaunted peers abroad. In the early 1950s the artist Kenneth Webb walked in our door and in 1968 we opened in Salthill the first commercially-built art gallery outside Dublin with an exhibition by Seán Keating. The gallery developed on the shoulders of these two giants and it opened our young minds to the world of artists and sculptors.

After we finished our formal education, five of us six children joined the business, each finding a niche. While Jane chose to pursue a career in teaching, she has never lost her deep interest in books and art. It is a testimony to the mutual devotion of our parents and their example of hard work that we have always worked well together as a team and that, almost forty years later, we are still involved in the business. Thomas, after a stint in the corner shop selling antiquarian maps and prints (earning the epithet 'the map man') took over management of the art gallery. Gerry trained to be a master bookbinder with J.H. Newman in Dublin and took over the book bindery which opened in 1974. Monica, with her natural pragmatism and eagle eye for figures, took charge of accounts. Conor's flexibility, versatility and determination are such that he has reinvented the firm at least twice.

My own apprenticeship to the trade was a long and curious one. From childhood we had all been fed an eclectic diet of reading material. My first visual memory is of Father walking towards my cot, his arms full of oranges and books. In the established tradition of this kind of memoir I must mention one incident from my school years that had a marked effect. My final-year French teacher didn't always adhere to traditional methods of teaching. His was the last class on Friday and on one occasion, surmising that our attention wasn't exactly avid, he told us to put our textbooks away and out of his pocket pulled a book which he considered essential reading for us. For the next number of weeks he was going to devote twenty minutes of class to it. He began to read J.D. Salinger's *The Catcher in the Rye*. In the context of the Ireland of 1966 this was, to say the least, innovative.

The more formal BA Course at University College Galway gave my literary education more focus. I then won a scholarship to the Sorbonne. My first months in Paris were lonely and I spent days scouring the second-hand bookshops on the Left Bank and the *bouquinistes* along the Seine for bargains. Once I had to sell some of my treasures to feed myself for a week. At night, to escape the confines of my *chambre de bonne* on the seventh floor, I came to know the cafés that allowed students to sit over a single *café espress* for two or three hours without comment. They provided warmth and a semblance of company and allowed me to read voraciously. This also cultivated in me the habit, never since lost, of reading in pubs.

In the summer of 1973 I returned to Galway after three years in Paris and joined Mother behind the counter in High Street. During my apprenticeship I can only remember receiving three formal pieces of advice from Mother. The first was that for every book in the shop there was a customer. My job was to marry them. The second instruction was to listen carefully to customers rather than prejudge what they might enjoy reading. The third came when I botched what would have been a significant sale. Rather than criticise me severely she simply said, 'You showed too much enthusiasm.' The rest of the business I learnt from her example and I was still learning when she retired at the age of eighty-six.

Father's contribution to my apprenticeship was different. He was an early riser and always started and finished work early. In his later years he would leave the shop about 3 pm, play some golf, or more likely walk the prom. He would then cook dinner and have the fire blazing and her drink poured for Mother when she arrived home. One day, I received a call from his desk: 'Select three books for me.' The next morning he told me that they were a load of rubbish. This continued for a number of months and I began to resent the calls, not only because I was busy (and why couldn't he select his own books?) but because of the slight on my ability to select books. But you rarely, if ever, said no to Father. Eventually there was a call that seriously irritated me and I took my anger out on the selection, putting more energy and thought into it. The following morning I heard, indirectly, that one of the books wasn't bad. I remembered the title and when the next call came through I used it as a basic reference. For a number of months, I got one right. One magical morning I was informed, indirectly as always, that two weren't bad and, although I never got three right, I felt I had passed a major test and I could finally call myself a bookseller. Father passed away in 1991 but even now when I am selecting books for one of our book-parcel clients I can sometimes feel his hand on my shoulder, guiding me.

The 1980s were a difficult time to be in the book trade. Conor felt that the future of the bookshop was in the United States. Since 1980 we had been the Irish vendor to the Library of Congress and in 1982 New York Public Libraries came on stream. Boston College was knocking at the door. In the spring of 1986 Father and Conor flew out on a three-week tour of Boston, Washington and New York. They went on a wing and a prayer. It proved to be a watershed for the bookshop.

Six months later Conor and I took another trip. For me it was an eye-opener, and any doubts about the market for Irish-interest books abroad were dispelled. After an exhausting two weeks we returned home with a briefcase full of orders but also with the realisation that our job, to echo Mother, was to put our books and their potential readers together.

Some time after that on a quiet afternoon I was towards the back of the shop cataloguing. Mother was behind the counter. An American walked in. He was at the end of his holiday, running out of cash, and he wanted us to mail a book to him. He examined the shelves, until suddenly he began to curse with some vehemence. Mother, ever a lady, started foostering under the counter and went into selective deafness.

I approached him with trepidation – he was a big man – and enquired, 'Excuse me sir, did we do something wrong?'

'It's not you,' he snorted. 'I am not a rich man. I can only come to Ireland once in a while. I love Irish books but I can get none at home. I walk into your shop and see all these wonderful books on your shelves. I want to bring the whole goddamned lot home and I can't.'

Mother's voice came sailing over the counter. 'We'll send you a parcel every so often.'

'You will?'

I can still see him turning to me, smiling.

'Of course we will,' I said.

The training I had received from the parents had kicked in. Unknown to myself I had been watching him at the shelves: 'You like this, you like that, you don't like this.'

Then he gave us the key: 'Here's my credit card number.' After that, every time a new book came in that reminded us of him, we added two or three more, billed them to his credit card and mailed them.

Soon there were two such customers. Then there were three. The Kenny's Personalised Book Club was born. As its membership increased, the club's *modus operandi* developed accordingly and is now firmly established: the suggestion to interested customers that they might like to receive book parcels by post; the frequency of the parcels – every two, three, four or six months; the budget per parcel; the profile of customers including their areas of interest, likes and dislikes. The books are sent on approval: a customer who doesn't like a book can return it. The one thing the recipient does not know is which books are in the package. No two selections are the same.

The first book parcels were sent out twenty years ago and now parcels go to over a thousand clients in every state of the Union and forty-five other countries worldwide.

This book is a celebration of the authors who wrote the 101 books I have selected. It is also a celebration of the publishers who published them, the publishers' representatives who introduced them to us, the customers who put their faith in us and the rich inheritance our parents have passed on to us. When

Currach Press agreed to publish this book I was overjoyed. Then I realised I was going to have to draw up a list and revisit again and again the 101 titles. Two problems presented themselves to me immediately – how to select 101 titles from among the thousands mailed to customers over the years, and what criteria would I use to determine the final choice? As Mother in her eighty-ninth year neatly put it: 'You're going to make somebody unhappy.'

These problems were exacerbated by the fact that a bookshop is the most democratic of places. Every writer whose work adorns its shelves deserves to be read. Every reader has individual tastes and different reasons for reading any particular title. The bookseller's job is to allow the author access to his or her audience and the reader access to the book that he or she will appreciate.

It is not a task to be taken lightly. There isn't and I hope there will never be the Ultimate Book. Every book should naturally lead to another on a continuing journey of discovery, adding an extra dimension to the reader's mental armoury. Some books reinforce cherished beliefs; others break the mould and can have a shattering effect on the reader. There are books that annoy, even infuriate. There are books that appeal on the first reading but fail to impress on the second – and vice versa. Furthermore, for no two individuals is the reading experience the same. This is what make the bookseller's job so challenging and exciting.

For this book I have selected titles that enhance the quality of life and that have a unique feel to them. My selection is informed by a personal belief that there are two essential ingredients to a good book: a story to be told and a writer who can tell it. The books selected here aren't necessarily the 101 'best' Irish books, if any such things as the 'best' books exist. There are of course omissions. I don't have to list them here as I have no doubt others will be quick to point them out. Nor are all the books in print. In fact some of them are quite difficult to source.

If I were to begin the selection again it would be significantly different. The fundamental criterion that determined this particular selection was the almost clichéd comment heard when people talk about books read or not read, or about favourite subjects or favourite authors: 'There is this book you *must* read.'

Taking all these elements into consideration I did what I normally do: I closed the file and went to the shelves. Then, in the same way as I would put together a package for a customer, I began to select 101 titles that would give a picture of Ireland's literary and cultural heritage.

The final selection has no rhyme or reason to it. It includes books that haven't been read for at least a generation as well as books that never got the attention they deserved. Some books were chosen not only because of their intrinsic merit but also because they represent an important aspect of Irish life and society. *Tá roinnt leabhar anseo freisin as Gaeilge.* Although the selection may not be – and did not set out to be – everybody's cup of tea, it is a celebration of the men and women who had the courage, skill and stamina to contribute to a magnificent tradition. It is also a tribute to two wonderful people who, as Seamus Heaney once put it, 'helped push the boat out' in their unique way – my parents Des and Maureen Kenny.

The creation of this book has been a fascinating journey with uphills, downhills, side streets, hidden laneways, cul de sacs, new vistas and some glorious surprises. It has never been boring or predictable. For those of you who have chosen to join me on the journey my sincere wish is that it will lead you to a new and exciting bibliographic treasure (or to renew your acquaintance with an old one). I hope that while you are reading this book you will enjoy at least one of those Eliotesque moments we all aspire to, the 'moment in and out of time'.

Des Kenny, August 2008

The Aran Islands

J. M. Synge

In our art gallery the first exhibition of photographs by Bill Doyle, featuring life on the Aran Islands, was remarkable for two reasons: the quality of the work itself and the public's reaction to it – in particular the reaction of the islanders. The exhibition contained a rather harrowing set of images of a child's coffin being made in one cottage and then carried on the handlebars of a bicycle to another. Some two weeks after the show opened, on an otherwise quiet afternoon, an elderly islander contemplated these images at length and then made the succinct comment: 'You know, the sea made great craftsmen of us all.'

This remark epitomises the world evoked in John Millington Synge's literary output and while he is rightly remembered as one of the major playwrights in Irish literature and a shining light of what is known as the Celtic Renaissance, his memoir of various visits to the Aran Islands, first published in 1908, is a prose classic.

Synge had been trying to make his way as a writer and literary critic in Paris without much success. The poet W.B. Yeats claims to have found him there struggling and suggested that he might serve his ambitions better by visiting the Aran Islands. This Synge did, making his first journey there in 1898.

That there was deep empathy between Synge and the islanders is immediately evident in the book, which begins with the now famous sentence: 'I am in Aranmor, sitting over a turf fire,

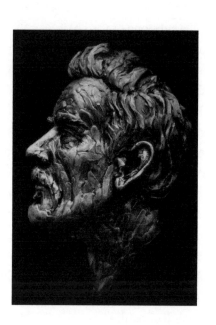

listening to a murmur of Gaelic that is rising from a little public house under my room.' The book continues in the same warm vein. The prose is concise and crystal-clear, allowing the reader to participate in the events, one of the charms of the book.

The world portrayed in the book is idyllic, almost Utopian. The natural hospitality of the islanders embraces the reader as much as it did the writer and they express a simple wisdom and a childlike curiosity about the outside world. To a large extent their world is now extinct, although traces of it still exist.

At the beginning of the book one Aranman tells us: 'I have seen Frenchmen and Danes and Germans…and there does be a power of Irish books along with them, and reading them better than ourselves. Believe me there are few rich men now in the world who are not studying Gaelic.'

This attitude was re-echoed recently by a weather forecaster on TG4, the Irish-language television station, when she announced, '*Seo aimsir an domhain. I Ros a'Mhíl, beidh sé ag cur báistí.*'

Thankfully, some things haven't changed!

Woodbrook

David Thomson

The name David Thomson may not feature in any biographical dictionary of Irish writers. However, Thomson's one book of Irish interest, *Woodbrook*, first published in 1974, has introduced more people to Ireland's political and social history than most.

The book defies classification. The latest paperback edition carries the following banner endorsement from Brian Moore: 'A brilliantly original mix of love story, memoir and history,' while Seamus Heaney tells us that '*Woodbrook* is simply one of the most enchanting books I've read in a long time...it begins in delight before it ends in wisdom.' Both these comments are justified, but they represent a simple overview of what *Woodbrook* is. They underline, however, that one of the extraordinary elements of this book is that it affects everyone in a different way, yet few can deny its charm.

Set in County Roscommon, between Boyle and Carrick-on-Shannon, from 1932 to just after the Second World War, it is a memoir of David Thomson (born in India of Scottish parents) who comes to Woodbrook Estate to tutor the two daughters of the Anglo-Irish landlords, the Kirkwoods.

He stays for ten years and falls in love, not only with the area but with the elder sister, Phoebe. To a large extent the book is a record of that rather unhappy love story but it is a whole lot more. There is the historical level: Thomson tells us how the Kirkwoods obtained the estate in the first place and how they managed to

David Thomson **Woodbrook**

hold on to it for just under three centuries. There are poignant descriptions of the Great Famine and its effect on the tenants and how these same tenants gradually acquired security of tenure and finally ownership of the land.

One of the more fascinating underlying tensions of the book is the struggle (albeit non-violent) between landlord and tenant for ownership of the land. As Thomson himself becomes more and more absorbed into the social fabric of the locality, he makes us acutely aware of the subtle differences between the landlord and the tenant, while never losing sight of their similarities. When eventually the changeover is made, the victory is not as sweet as had been dreamt of and the tenant finds himself locked into the same despair as his erstwhile landlord.

Woodbrook is a love story but it also has all the elements of classical tragedy as the 'relics of auld decency' make way for the new landlords in the fledgling independent Irish state.

Puckoon

Spike Milligan

Like David Thomson, Spike Milligan rarely features in reference books relating to Irish literature. He was born in India and educated there and in England. His only connection with Ireland was his father, who hailed from Sligo. At one stage Milligan was refused an English passport, an event which made him acutely aware of his Irish background.

Puckoon, one of the funniest Irish books ever, is set on the Sligo-Fermanagh border. It is an unadulterated attack on English imperialism and lampoons the almost drunken way in which the partition of Ireland was effected. The border between the North and South was so haphazard that there were cases where you could walk in the front door of a house a citizen of the Republic of Ireland and out the back door a subject of His or Her Majesty.

When the book was first published in 1963, the censorship laws ensured that it received little recognition in Ireland and was more difficult to find than *Ulysses* (which despite a much-publicised trial concerning its publication in the US, was never actually banned in Ireland).

The only real chance of acquiring a copy of *Puckoon* was to find a man in the sleazy gabardine coat whose inside pocket had a well-thumbed copy of the book along with the 'feelthy pictures'.

After some years of growing sales in this manner there emerged in Irish society a cult called 'Puckooners.' At first they were considered a dangerous breed who recognised each other

by two left-eye twitches, the answer to which was two right-eye twitches. Their general meeting places were public lavatories and down-and-nearly-out public houses (female Puckooners resorted to cordial parlours down the hallways of the same down-and-nearly-out public houses).

With the relaxing of the censorship laws – which of course hadn't banned *Puckoon* – there was a prolonged and passionate debate in the Dáil, the Senate and St Patrick's College, Maynooth, as to whether this notorious book should be released on the innocent, holy, apostolic and Catholic population of Ireland without a health warning. It was feared that not only would it be a danger to the political and religious morals of the population without a health warning – the Protestants didn't count – but that it would reveal certain skulduggeries as practised by the Holders of High Office in Ireland which the population might be better off not hearing about. Only the threat made by the Communist Party of Ireland that its entire membership – six in all – would invade all Sunday Masses just as the sermons were beginning prevented this from happening, thereby earning our undying gratitude.

Home Before Night

HUGH LEONARD

As an opening line, 'My grandmother made dying her life's work' has few equals. As a tender and loving tribute to adoptive parents, *Home Before Night* has even fewer.

Hugh Leonard, the pseudonym of John Keyes Byrne, was in fact born to a single mother in Dublin in 1926. He was adopted into the family that features in *Home Before Night* and brought up in Dalkey. At the age of nineteen he joined the civil service, where he was to remain for fourteen years before becoming a full-time writer. During his tenure he was involved in amateur dramatics. His play *The Big Birthday was* produced in 1956 by the Abbey, followed by a production of *Madigan's Lock* in 1958. Leonard then moved to Manchester, where he worked for Granada Television. He began his life-long relationship with the Dublin Theatre Festival in 1960, the year his play *A Walk in the Water* was produced. Although Leonard's bread-and-butter work was in film and television he became renowned in Ireland for his stage plays, many of which were produced in the Abbey, and as a man of letters. Perhaps his most famous play was *Da*, in which he revisited his Dalkey childhood. *Da* became a Broadway hit in 1978.

Leonard's work as a dramatist, satirist, adapter of Joyce and Plunkett and script-writer for television and film has often overshadowed his powerful autobiographical volume *Home Before Night*, first published in 1979.

With remarkable skill and deft use of language, Leonard

draws us into the hearth of Nicholas and Margaret Keyes and the world of 1930s Dalkey. Adopting the Balzacian technique of the ever-widening circle ('Growing older can be measured by playgrounds') he brings us from childhood through to adulthood with tears and laughter, innocence and discovery, very little money and a great deal of humanity. The whole is imbued with deep parental affection.

A major feature of the book is Leonard's avoidance of sentimentality. He achieves this through inspired prose, an exquisite use of one-liners ('Our dog, Jack, was anti-clerical') and an overall gruffness which hardly camouflages aspects of his adoptive family's kindness. This is especially evident in the flow of warmth and devotion beautifully and lyrically penned on the last page.

In the generation following its publication, *Home Before Night* has acquired a deeper meaning. Ireland has been awash with revelations of abuse and neglect in orphanages and children's homes throughout the country. Institutions have been subjected to a severe examination and exposed as having been less than Christian and humane in discharging their duties.

In *Home Before Night,* by acknowledging the full and decent childhood he experienced, Leonard pays tribute not only to the generosity of his adoptive parents who opened their hearts and home to him but to the countless other couples who did likewise for the children they adopted. The book is not just a delightful read, it is a powerful testimony to their humanity.

The Heather Blazing

COLM TÓIBÍN

There is in Colm Tóibín's second novel *The Heather Blazing* a sense of coming of age, a path that had to be taken by the author (and in a larger sense Ireland) before he could achieve the accomplishments of his later novels, *The Blackwater Lightship* and *The Master*. In taking this path, Tóibín honestly and courageously dismantles the shackles placed on him and his generation by the conservative and Catholic Ireland of the pre-1970s, ridding himself of the barriers to self-knowledge. The pain of this journey is symbolised in the book by the fact that it takes four generations to achieve an honest degree of personal freedom.

Born in Wexford in 1955 and educated at University College Dublin, Tóibín began working as a journalist. His first book *Walking Along the Border* was a remarkable account of the daily lives of the people living on the border between the North of Ireland and the Republic at the height of the Troubles. Another non-fiction book *Homage to Barcelona* testified to his affection for Spain.

His first novel, *The South*, published in 1990, was set in Spain and Wexford. It was, however, with the publication of *The Heather Blazing* in 1993 that he first made his mark as a writer of note. Since then he has carved out a serious international reputation as one of the finest novelists writing in the English language today.

Set in Wexford and Dublin, *The Heather Blazing* is the story of Eamon Redmond, a high-court judge and a supporter of the status quo. Using a flashback technique and the shadow of

the 1798 rebellion, Tóibín unravels his hero's life and character, peeling away the personal and professional props that Redmond has mounted to protect himself from his own humanity. The narration is imbued with a delightful contrast between the pomp of Redmond's high judicial office and the down-to-earth domesticity of his home life.

One of the more enjoyable elements of the book is Tóibín's growing confidence and skill as a novelist. There is a draughtsman-like structure to the novel and a fluidity of language. His use of the characters around Redmond to highlight his strengths and weaknesses is intriguing – particularly Carmel, Redmond's wife, whose stroke is the *deus ex machina* of the novel.

The Heather Blazing epitomises the transition of the old Ireland of the 1950s and 1960s to the new Ireland of the end of the twentieth century. In the old the twin crutches of Church and nationality were the arbitrators of our behaviour and aspirations, while in the new the individual is more often than not the sole arbitrator of his or her own destiny, as defined by personal experience and natural inclinations. In this respect Tóibín's novel was as important step for a country aspiring to cultural maturity.

The Big Chapel

Tom Kilroy

There is a number of books in the Irish literary canon that stand completely alone without comparison to anything that preceded or followed them, that have no reference to time, place or author but which are unmistakably Irish. These books seem to be the spontaneous expression of a story that could not be left untold, of an event that would not be suppressed no matter how severe the censorship but that would find its way into the public domain come hell or high water. Such a book is *The Big Chapel* by Tom Kilroy.

Born in Callan, County Kilkenny in 1934, Kilroy became one of Ireland's leading dramatists following the production of his first successful play *The Death and Resurrection of Mr Roche* in 1969. He wrote this play while he was a lecturer at University College Dublin. Kilroy taught at a number of American universities before becoming Professor of English at University College Galway in 1978. However his first love was the theatre and he served as play editor to the Abbey in 1977. He was appointed a director of Field Day in 1988. His two most successful plays were possibly *Talbot's Box* and *Double Cross*, and he adapted Chekov's *The Seagull*, situating his version in the West of Ireland. *The Big Chapel*, published in 1971, is his only novel.

The book is based on a nineteenth-century scandal that took place in County Kilkenny and relates the story of what happened when the local bishop proposed to replace a village

school with another run by the Christian Brothers. The parish priest resists and the resident teacher sides with him. This situation splits the village into two factions, provoking riot, arson and finally murder.

The book is about the struggle for power and the polarising effect such a struggle can have on a small rural community. By using a country town as the location, Kilroy succeeds in creating a well-defined demographic entity and this allows him to explore the dispute across all the social strata, much the same technique as that used by Albert Camus in *La Peste*.

Due to this concentration, Kilroy achieves an intensity of emotion from which the narration derives tremendous energy. The book moves to its conclusion with the inevitability of Greek tragedy and the few moments of human love or affection that occur in the story are soon overwhelmed and annihilated. The novel has an extreme and fatal sense of victimisation that is almost unbearable.

The conflict between individuality and the autocratic desire for organisation, whether it be religious, social, economic, political or cultural, continues in many aspects of Irish life and is a recurrent theme in the country's literature. Few deal with it as thoroughly or as forcefully from the beginning of the conflict through to the (nearly always) inevitable and humiliating defeat of the individual spirit as Tom Kilroy does in *The Big Chapel*.

The Ikon Maker

DESMOND HOGAN

On a bright summer's morning in 1972, two gallant young gentle-men presented themselves before the counter of our bookshop in High Street, Galway. As Mother spoke to them it emerged that each of them had just had his first book published, one a novel and the other a collection of short stories, by a new press called Co-op Books which they themselves along with some friends had set up in Dublin. They were on a selling mission to Galway and wanted to know if we would be interested in stocking copies.

Mother asked to look at the books and after a summary perusal enquired if they had any more copies with them. It transpired that they had about twenty copies of each book which they hoped to sell before day's end.

'Well,' said Mother, 'your day's work is now finished, I'll take them all, but I would be most grateful if you two gentlemen would sign them.'

Sign them! There followed wild and wonderful jubilation. Pens were produced, cameras went click, click and for the best part of an hour there were scenes of celebration in the shop.

Strangely, the record of that event is one of the few black-and-white photos that hang in the Kenny Pantheon. It certainly is one of the happiest, and while the two gentlemen in question have gained considerable international recognition since then, for Mother, film director and novelist Neil Jordan and short-story writer Desmond Hogan would always be 'the two lads'.

Something else beyond the welcoming of two new authors on to the Irish literary scene happened that summer. Irish writing crossed a serious threshold. While Neil Jordan has since concentrated more on his film work, with an Oscar or two to his credit, Desmond Hogan went on to become for many, to quote Jennifer Johnston, 'the finest novelist writing in Ireland throughout the twentieth century'.

Hogan was born in Ballinasloe, County Galway, in 1950 and attended national and secondary school there before going to University College Dublin. He won a Hennessy award in 1971 and his play, *A Short Walk to the Sea*, was staged in the Peacock Theatre in Dublin in 1975. The publication of *The Ikon Maker* a year later established him firmly as a writer of note.

Hogan's prose has a curious magnetic effect. Its hypnotic lyricism draws the reader into the heart of the story. In *The Ikon Maker* Hogan evokes a dreamlike pastoral landscape, contrasting it with the stark realities of the emigrant's life in industrial England during the grim 1970s. Wonderful use of language strengthens the narrative while the author's empathy for his anti-hero is always evident.

The novel is a powerful introduction to Hogan's work. It deals with loss, regeneration and the juxtaposition of two generations who just seem to keep passing each other in the dark. It epitomises the Ireland of the 1970s, a country that was confused but shedding its insularity.

Waiting for Godot

Samuel Beckett

The enigma of *Waiting for Godot* is that it is about Nothing At All and Everything At Once. It is the most quintessentially universal play about Everyman in any language and the essentially Irish play about Nobody. It is an atheistic play about spirituality. It does nothing and achieves everything. It is static and mobile. It is stripped in language but rich in meaning and resonance. It is imbued with deep compassion and pathos, yet devoid of sentiment. You can take it as a tragic comedy or a comic tragedy. You can take it any way you like but it will definitely touch a chord deep within you.

It could only have been written by Samuel Beckett.

Born in Foxrock, County Dublin in 1906, the second son of a quantity surveyor, Samuel Beckett was educated at Portora Royal School in Enniskillen and at Trinity College Dublin. He taught French at Campbell College Belfast and was a Lecteur d'Anglais at the Ecole Normale Supérieure in Paris. It was during this first period in Paris that he met James Joyce through his friendship with the poet Thomas MacGreevy. His first publication, in 1929, was *Dante...Bruno...Vico...Joyce.*

Beckett lived in various parts of Europe during the 1930s before settling in Paris in 1937. During the Second World War he became involved with the French Resistance and managed to escape when his cell was betrayed. He was awarded the Croix de Guerre in 1945. In that year he decided to write in French to

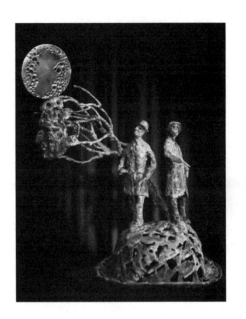

purify his style. *Waiting for Godot* was written in 1948 and 1949. Beckett won the Nobel Prize in 1969. He died in 1989.

The inherent attraction of *Waiting for Godot* is its unexpectedness. No matter how the play is approached, it surprises and bewilders. For all its darkness and apparent gloom, it has moments of extraordinary lightness and delightful humour. From its famous opening line, 'Nothing to be done,' to its indecisive conclusion, 'Let's go (they do not move),' it is brimful with an almost impish irony.

Yet, for all the philosophical debates it has inspired, for the hundreds of books of literary criticism it has generated, for the thousands of interpretations of its texts that have been done, there is a deep subliminal humanity within the play that is as elusive of definition as its manifestations are unexpected and refreshing – especially when these manifestations are close to home.

In the last six months of Father's final illness, *Waiting for Godot* was Mother's bedtime reading. In a time of deep personal stress, she derived tremendous consolation and strength from the play and concluded that Beckett must have had a close relative with an illness similar to Father's. She was intensely grateful for his understanding and his kindness.

The achievement of *Waiting for Godot* on the personal as well as aesthetic level is surely one of the great wonders of Irish literature.

The Hard Road to Klondike

MICÍ MAC GABHANN

The Hard Road to Klondike is a modest but powerful book. It combines the best of the oral storytelling tradition with a strong direct narrative. The result is one of the great unsung masterpieces of the Irish storyteller's art in print. First published in the Irish language with the title *Rotha Mór an tSaoil*, it was translated by Valentin Iremonger and the English version was published in 1962.

Micí Mac Gabhann was born in 1865 in the parish of Cloghaneeley in Gweedore, County Donegal, the eldest of twelve children. The book is the story of the first forty years of his extraordinary life, as narrated to his son-in-law shortly before his death in 1948.

Over those four decades, Mac Gabhann witnesses the harshness of landlord law, is hired out at the age of eight to Lagan farmers for a couple of seasons, walks the fifty miles to Derry where he takes the 'Derryboat' as a seasonal migrant to Scotland, crosses the Atlantic and works in Bethlehem, Pennsylvania and Butte, Montana, before joining the Gold Rush to the Klondike. After a long, arduous and adventurous journey across America and up the Yukon River to Dawson City, he reaches the gold fields, where, having endured great hardship, he strikes gold. After all that, and with a fine sense of destiny, he retraces his steps home to Donegal where he gets married and raises a family.

The real magic of the book is the narrative itself. From the

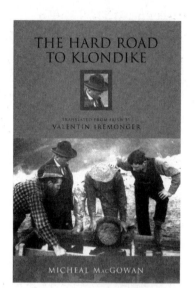

THE HARD ROAD
TO KLONDIKE

TRANSLATED FROM IRISH BY
VALENTIN IREMONGER

MICHEAL MacGOWAN

beginning the pace is even and unassuming, lacking any sense of self-pity, especially when Mac Gabhann is describing the hardships of being an eight-year-old servant boy. With the art of the seasoned storyteller he writes, 'Repetition makes a story dull and I'll say no more about that.'

We learn that, 'it wasn't hard to get to America at the time. You only had to go to Derry and get on the boat – so long as you had the money, there was no trouble about it.' However, things aren't as easy as they seem and, after a tough crossing and a year in Pennsylvania, we are told '…between hard work and low pay, I thought no more of America than I did of Scotland. Everyone you met was trying to get more out of you than the next person and as bad as life was in Scotland, it wasn't much better in America.'

In fact, Mac Gabhann finds himself almost destitute when the news of the Klondike Gold Strike comes through and he and some companions decide to take the gamble and go there. The trip up the Yukon reads like a Hammond Innes or Alistair MacLean thriller. From the moment we leave San Francisco, the tempo goes up a gear. Although the prose remains even, Mac Gabhann instills a new excitement into the story that enthrals and engages.

In *The Hard Road to Klondike*, the reader hears every syllable and shares in the experience although he or she never leaves the proverbial fireplace. In any language, it would be a rare gem of a book.

Like Any Other Man

Patrick Boyle

Patrick Boyle was born in Ballymoney, County Antrim, in 1905. He was educated in the Coleraine Academical Institution, after which he was employed by the Ulster Bank. He remained on the bank's payroll for forty-five years, ending up as a bank manager in County Wexford, but for the greater part of forty-five years' service he was based in County Donegal, where most of his stories are set. He began to write in his forties, publishing his first collection *At Night All Cats are Grey* in 1966. His stories are marked by dark humour and incisive satire, which earned him a considerable literary reputation during the 1960s and 1970s. Nowadays he is almost forgotten. He died in 1982.

Patrick Boyle may be considered primarily a short-story writer, but his most significant literary achievement is his only novel *Like Any Other Man*, which was published in 1966. Using the biblical tale of Samson and Delilah as his model, Boyle reveals the aridity and fragility of small-town 1950s Ireland, built, as it was, on the twin pillars of hypocrisy and guilt. From the first page the atmosphere is imbued with the dishonesty and deceit endemic in every stratum of the local community.

Jim Simpson is the local bank manager. Physically big and strong, he is in more ways than one the most powerful man in town. He is also the most vulnerable. In the opening passage we find him late for work, badly hungover but using his position as manager to conceal his weaknesses. Feeling a constant need to

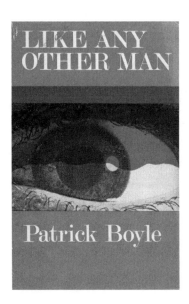

LIKE ANY
OTHER MAN

Patrick Boyle

prove himself, he indulges in almost daily drinking bouts during which he often performs feats of physical strength to bolster his self-image as the town's most powerful man. During one of these bouts, he meets Delia, the publican's visiting niece.

What begins as a purely physical relationship rapidly becomes an obsession. Simpson's inability to deal with the situation results in even more savage drinking bouts, ocular haemorrhages leading to impending blindness, unreasonable jealousies, near insanity and his own and Delia's destruction.

A remarkable feature of the novel is the sheer intensity of the prose, particularly the descriptions of the drinking bouts which are so vivid that you can almost smell the alcohol. One of the more memorable passages is the one describing Simpson's increasing insomnia and underlying fear, symbolised by his pathological obsession with the tick-tock of real and imaginary clocks. The passage is strongly reminiscent of the paranoia suffered by the protagonist in 'Le Horla', Guy de Maupassant's short story about approaching insanity.

As Boyle's novel moves to its inevitable conclusion, the intensity increases. Simpson's weaknesses become more marked and he flounders helplessly and lashes at all around him in a vain attempt to regain equilibrium and self-respect.

Thy Tears Might Cease

Michael Farrell

Born in 1899 of well-to-do parents, Michael Farrell was reared in Carlow. He studied medicine in University College Dublin, where he became involved in the nationalist movement and spent some time in prison during the War of Independence for possession of illegal documents. After being released from prison he went on a long walking tour of the Continent and thereafter to the Belgian Congo. He returned to Ireland in 1930 and resumed his medical studies, this time in Trinity College, but then moved to Wicklow where, in 1932, he abandoned medicine and began work on what became known in Irish literary circles for the next thirty years as 'The Great Irish Novel'.

While his novel continued to grow and grow, both in reality and in literary myth, Farrell became a regular contributor to the *The Bell* magazine as theatre correspondent and columnist under the pseudonym 'Lemuel Gulliver'.

By the 1950s his novel had reached gigantic proportions but Farrell could never bring himself to edit it or allow anyone else to do so. It remained unpublished when he died in 1962. At his widow's request, Monk Gibbon, a family friend, edited the manuscript and in 1963 the novel was finally published. Entitled *Thy Tears Might Cease*, it was an immediate success.

The novel is a glorious pain in the ass. It's a pain in the ass because it was published almost despite itself – taking as it did thirty years to be written, with its author refusing to edit it even

THY TEARS MIGHT CEASE

Michael Farrell

though it had a publisher, and having to wait until after its author's death to see the light of day.

It's a pain in the ass because it is a novel with an introduction and an attitude. Novels with introductions are suspect. Like the rugby forward who plucks the ball out of the skies with what appears to be an amazing leap, such a novel couldn't exist without an introduction, just as the forward couldn't make the leap without two other forwards lifting him off the ground. Novels with attitude are best left in manuscript form.

It's a pain in the ass because it stands there, in 1963, a huge monolith of a Victorian novel written at a time when it was thought that the Victorian novel with all its sighs and cries, its moans and groans, should remain in the university lecture halls among academics justifying their professional existence by trotting out literary study after literary study.

It's a pain in the ass because no matter how you try to dodge it, it deserves its place in any Irish library although it is almost impossible to say why. The text is often turgid, the pace sluggish, and then, all of a sudden, the narration takes off like a bat out of hell, seducing the reader into believing that the struggle up to now has been worthwhile – until the next lump of undigested prose.

In 1963, *Thy Tears Might Cease* was like a breath of fresh air. Curiously, since then it has been rarely out of print. At a time when the 1916 hagiography was just beginning to gather momentum in preparation for the fiftieth anniversary of the Easter Rebellion, it was a voice of reason sounding in the wilderness. Michael Farrell may not have achieved all he had intended in the novel but he certainly went a long, long way towards it.

Over Nine Waves

Marie Heaney

A late autumn afternoon in 1960. The boys file into class. An elderly teacher follows them, shuts the door and makes his way to the top of the room. He places his bits and pieces on the table, turns, faces the boys, puts his thumbs in his braces and, in a solemn base voice, intones: '*Tá scéal sa bhéaloideas gur tháinig cúig chlainne daoine go hÉirinn.*'

At the age of ten, sitting in the back row of Rang a Ceathair, Coláiste Iognáid, I was listening to my first formal history lesson and a world of magic and wonder was opened to me.

No matter how you approach it, each country's history begins with its mythology. Of its nature, however, mythology has no chronology and the individual's experience of it tends to be haphazard, which is fine in its own way, but incomplete.

There are four cycles of Irish mythology: the Mythological Cycle, the Cycle of Kings, the Ulster Cycle and the Fianna Cycle. The most complete of these is the Ulster Cycle, encapsulated in the epic tale known as the *Táin Bó Cuailgne*. There are also the Three Sorrows of Irish storytelling, 'The Children of Lir,' 'Deirdre of the Sorrows,' and, 'The Children of Turenn'.

Most books of Irish mythology have tended to emphasise the more popular stories, such as how Cúchulainn got his name, or how Fionn Mac Cumhail first tasted the Salmon of Knowledge, and therefore give an incomplete picture of the full extent and development of the Irish mythological tradition.

Then, in 1994, Faber and Faber published *Over Nine Waves, A Book of Irish Legends* by Marie Heaney.

Born in County Tyrone, Marie Heaney trained as a teacher in Belfast and began her career in schools in Northern Ireland. She graduated with an M.Phil from University College Dublin in 1997, and in her capacity as editor for Town House publishers she edited a number of anthologies of poetry and short prose essays. She now lives in Dublin with her husband and they have three adult children. In her own writing, she has a special interest in Irish mythology.

In *Over Nine Waves*, Maire Heaney goes a considerable way towards giving us a comprehensive account at Irish mythology. She begins with the routing of the Fir Bolg by the magical Tuatha Dé Danann and works her way through the invasions of Ireland until it is finally settled by the Milesians. These tales are followed by the Ulster Cycle, which is basically the story of the Brown Bull of Cooley and the great warrior Cúchulainn, the adventures of Fionn Mac Cumhail and the Fianna and the coming of Christianity. She finishes with the legends of the three patron saints of Ireland, Patrick, Brigid and Colmcille.

Two pleasing aspects of this book are the consistency of the narration and the even pace of the prose. These give the book a unity that is somehow lacking in other books of its kind and make *Over Nine Waves* the most complete and informative book of Irish mythology to date. It is a delightful read.

The Rough Field

John Montague

'Poets,' John Montague once remarked in our High Street bookshop, as he noted the prices on some scarce out-of-print poetry collections, 'are like dumb blonds. They don't know the riches they are sitting on until it is too late.'

Certainly, that was one fault that Montague himself could never be accused of. When it was published in 1972, *The Rough Field* became the first poetry bestseller in our experience. In fact, for ever after, Mother always remembered that Christmas as being 'The Christmas of *The Rough Field*' and, in the same way that events in 19th-century Ireland were dated by whether they occurred before or after the Big Wind of 1839, every Irish poetry collection was remembered as having been published either before or after Montague's most important work.

Born in 1929 in Brooklyn, New York, Montague was raised from the age of four by two aunts in Garvaghey, County Tyrone. He was educated at Saint Patrick's College, Armagh, University College Dublin and Yale University. He lived in Paris for a period before going to the United States, where he taught at Berkeley University. He returned to Ireland in 1972 to take up an academic position at University College Cork from which he retired as Associate Professor of English. In 1998, he was the first poet to be appointed to the Ireland Chair of Poetry.

The book, the title of which is a version of the townland name Garvaghey *(Garbh Fhaiche)* is made up of ten poetic sequences,

most of which had been previously published in various forms. The tenor of the collection is established in the first sequence 'Home Again' with the lines:

> Rough Field is the Gaelic and rightly named
> As setting for a mode of life that passes on:
> Harsh landscape that haunts me,
> Well and stone, in the black moons of dream,
> With all my circling a failure to return.

His coming to Ulster, yet again, inspires a meditation on the Montagues' first arrival in the province. Their history and apparently lost traditions still reach and haunt him through many generations:

> Twenty years afterwards, I saw the church again
> And promised to remember my burly grandfather
> And his rural craft, after this fashion
> So succession passes, through strangest hands.

Montague also pays tribute to his childhood neighbours and mentors, acknowledging their influence on his spiritual make-up: 'Like dolmens round my childhood, the old people'.

Having identified the importance of the symbols and traditions of the past as an essential ingredient in the Irish ethos, Montague also recognises that Ireland in 1972 was on the cusp of spiritual and cultural change: 'Puritan Ireland's dead and gone/A myth of O'Connor and O'Faolain.'

The Rough Field is a magnificent collection and Montague's greatest achievement.

The All of It

JEANETTE HAIEN

You could be excused for not seeing this book as being Irish. Published in 1986 by that wonderful Boston publishing company David Godine, the novel could be taken as American, English, French or anything else you fancy. It was also published in England by Faber and Faber but received little or no notice on this side of the Atlantic.

The blurb tells us that the author is well known in the US and in Europe as a concert pianist and teacher. It adds that she and her husband, a lawyer, live in Manhattan and spent a fraction of each year at their summer home in Connemara.

The book, except for a few language slips, is, however, indisputably Irish and ranks as one of the more lyrical and moving novels set in the west of Ireland. As Benedict Kiely puts it: 'Whenever and wherever Jeanette Haien came upon the germ of this story, or was blessed with a vision of it, then and there she came upon a jewel.'

From the first sentence, which begins –

> Thomas Dunn, the head ghillie at the Castle, wasn't telling Father Declan anything he didn't already know: the river too high and wild from all the rains, and the salmon, therefore, not moving, just lying on the bottom, not showing themselves at all, and the midges terrible, and only two days left to the season so of course all but

the least desirable of the river-beats, number four, was
let already;…'

to the last:

He called out again, 'Goodnight Enda.' Then turned
the wheel hard to the right and started off down the
moonlit lane.'

– the reader is riveted.

Father Declan de Loughrey is in a difficult moral bind: Kevin,
a hard-working small farmer in his parish has just died. At his
deathbed, his partner, a beautiful energetic woman called Enda,
confesses to the priest that Kevin is not in fact her husband at all
but her brother, and that they have been living in an incestuous
relationship for more than forty years.

This presents a major moral problem for the priest: Kevin
and Enda have been devout Catholics and fervent Mass goers,
and Enda wants a proper and decent funeral to which, because
of their illegal relationship, Kevin has no right. This dilemma is
exacerbated as Enda tells the whole story – or the all of it.

The storyline is strong and the writing is delicately paced.
Haien's skill in handling the narrative is one of the great joys of
the book. Her feeling for the Connemara and Mayo landscape
is exquisite and she imbues the apparently tragic portent of the
book with deft touches of humour.

Only towards the end of the novel does the real theme appear.
The All of It is a rare gem of a book and deserves a lot more interest
than it has ever received.

The Last of the Name

CHARLES MCGLINCHY

'Clonmany! You drive as far as Malin Head and then reverse ten mile.' These were the directions Thomas received as he answered an invitation to an extraordinary book launch. It's the loneliest place on earth for a book launch, yet the most appropriate for *The Last of the Name*, which evolved from its very fields, stones and people.

Charles McGlinchy, a weaver, was past his nineties in the late 1940s and realising that his end was approaching with no kith or kin, began to relate his life to Patrick Kavanagh, the local school principal. Kavanagh recorded everything in the same school copybooks his students used.

McGlinchy died in 1954 and Kavanagh put the copybooks away, conscious that the material was not yet appropriate for public consumption. A generation later, his son Desmond, who had always felt that something should be done about the manuscripts, showed them to his old classmate and lifelong friend Seamus Heaney. Heaney said, yes, this was a classic but felt that Brian Friel was perhaps better placed to understand the spirit of the text and turn it into a book. Friel undertook the task and the result was launched in Clonmany in 1986.

The book is descriptive. From the outset we are listening to the voice of an old man who, in two simple sentences, transports us back two hundred years. The tone is so intimate that all concept of time and place is lost and the magic that is being woven around us is so enthralling that, by page five, we are chewing this man's

tobacco and by page ten we are spitting into the fire with him.

For the next two hours we become participants in the daily life of rural Ireland over two centuries. Our grandfather is press-ganged into the British navy to fight Napoleon; our neighbours deal with an amorous landlord in a crude but effective way; our local police pour seized poteen down a drain in front of the sergeant from Buncrana (only to enjoy it to the full with the neighbours that evening); our curate the Waterloo priest spends a quarter in prison for refusing to pay tithes; with Seán Crossach we hold up the coach of the landlord's agent, fooling him into believing there are more than one of us robbing him; and we hear that the Great Hunger of 1847 wasn't a patch on the famine of the 'Dear Summer' of 1817.

The panorama of two centuries passes before our eyes but the real magic of the book is that we never leave McGlinchy's fireside. While the principal aim of its author was to have these things written down for posterity – for even then it was recognised that change was inevitable and that most of the old ways and customs would be lost forever – the book takes on a life and vigour of its own and as the old man's voice wraps us in its warmth we realise that we are witnessing one of the classic descriptions of the Irish cultural experience.

Rain on the Wind

Walter Macken

Published in 1950, *Rain on the Wind* has captured the minds and hearts of its readers in a way that few other books have done. There are people who still talk wistfully about the wonderful sunny day when, sitting on a bench on the promenade in Salthill, they opened the book for the first time and read the famous first line: 'A big grey gander it was.'

Rain on the Wind was created by the quintessential Galway writer, Walter Macken. He was born in Galway in 1915 and spent most of his life there. From an early age he became involved in Galway's Irish-language theatre, An Taibhdhearc, where he was manager, actor, translator, producer and general dogsbody. However, his plays in English, beginning with *Mungo's Mansions* in 1946, won him a wider recognition and he became known as Galway's Seán O'Casey.

Macken's first novel *Quench the Moon* was published in 1948 but it was *Rain on the Wind* that firmly established him as a master fiction writer, a reputation that was to be confirmed by the famous historical trilogy: *Seek the Fair Land*, *The Silent People* and *The Scorching Wind*. He died in 1967.

The storyline of *Rain on the Wind* follows the classic rich man/poor man path. We are introduced to the household of Gran, son Mhicil, daughter-in-law Delia and their two sons Tommy and Mico. We are never given (nor ever need) a character's surname. Of the two sons, Tommy is the mother's favourite and she never

tires of telling the world this. He is tall, handsome and hugely successful at school and university. Mico, on the other hand, is blemished with a birth mark that covers one side of his face, fails miserably at school and is, according to Delia, the cause of all the family's troubles.

However, Mico, for all his clumsiness and apparent stupidity, is kind, gentle and caring. His one wish is to follow his grandfather's and father's steps as a fisherman. He has the natural talents of a boatman. This is further anathema to his mother who sees nothing but grinding poverty as the fisherman's lot. Add Peter, the brilliant student, Jo his girlfriend, Pa the venerable and feared teacher, Twacky, Padneen, Uncle James from Connemara, Coimín and Maeve, also from Connemara, and you have the full cast.

The story moves from the Claddagh, the famed fishing village adjacent to the city of Galway, to the shores of Connemara, to the prehistoric fort of Dún Aengus on Inis Mór. The pace of the narrative never loses dramatic power and the reader is treated to scene after memorable scene, For some readers the most memorable scene it is the opening passage with the three-year-old Mico and his elder brother being chased across the Swamp by a gaggle of geese; for others it is the night spent by our heroes on an island invaded by rats. Then there is the remarkable description of the hurling match, the haunting appearance of the ghost ship and the spectacular storm scene.

The real achievement of the book is that Macken, while staying on top of his narrative, never loses sight of the spectacular scenery of Galway Bay and Connemara as the story moves seamlessly to its conclusion.

Without my Cloak

KATE O'BRIEN

During the late 1950s or early 1960s Kate O'Brien lived in Roundstone. Every two months or so she would take the bus into Galway to meet her publisher for lunch in the Great Southern Hotel. She would get off the bus at the Spanish Arch and would generally drop in to Mother to say hello on the way to her meeting.

Some hours later Kate would come sailing down High Street, open the door with a flourish and announce with pomp and ceremony: 'Here comes Kate, full of port,' whereupon, as the family legend has it, she would pick up a book of poetry and read aloud with gusto the bawdiest poem therein.

This rather bohemian image of Kate O'Brien contrasted sharply with the darker, austere image of the severe-looking woman as portrayed in nearly all the photographs of the writer.

There is no doubt, however, that Kate O'Brien is one of the finest novelists ever to come out of Ireland. Not only does she tell a great story well: her technical approach and the quality of her writing leave her second to none in her field.

Unfortunately, no other writer – with the possible exception of Edna O'Brien – was made to suffer such vilification and ostracism at the hands of her own people because of her craft.

In modern terms, *Without my Cloak* would be described as a family saga, full of lust and greed, spanning four generations, covering three continents. It is this and a whole lot more: it is a

book about the independent human spirit trying to express itself in a stultifying and morally stale society. It is about the loneliness suffered by that spirit of independence and its one act of rebellion before it must finally submit to the mores of the society it lives in.

The Considine family are the epitome of respectability in the town of Mellick, their power, wealth and status built on the shoulders of 'Honest John'. It is indicative of O'Brien's sense of humour and irony that the founder of this dynasty is a horse thief. This fact has been firmly buried and the Considines are now on the verge of becoming the most respectable and wealthy family in the town.

To their great consternation, there are individuals within the family (Caroline in the third and Denis in the fourth generation) who do not act in the respectable manner expected of them and the action (and energy) of the novel revolves around their one act of rebellion.

First published in 1931, this novel was a serious act of rebellion in itself. O'Brien was questioning the hypocritical respectability in which Ireland was enveloping itself. Her own independent spirit never conformed to that society. She died in poverty in 1974.

Never No More

MAURA LAVERTY

Maura Laverty is remembered today, if she is remembered at all, for her cookbook *All in the Cooking*. However, for two decades following its publication in 1942, there were few homes in Ireland that didn't have a copy of her book *Never No More*. Generally called a novel, *Never No More* is possibly the first in the tradition of the rural memoir that later found its modern voice in Alice Taylor.

Maura Laverty was born Maura Kelly in Rathangan, County Kildare, in 1907 and spent her childhood with her grandmother at Derrymore House. After training as a teacher in Brigidine House, County Carlow she went to Spain in 1925 to work as a governess. Treated badly by her employers and ostracised by her fellow governesses, she was fortunate to meet and become the secretary to Princess Bibesco. Later she became a journalist in Madrid before returning to Ireland to continue her career in journalism and broadcasting. *Never No More* was her first book and was followed by several more, including the highly popular cookbooks. She was also the scriptwriter for the RTÉ series *Tolka Row*. She died in 1967.

The book opens with the funeral of the narrator's (Delia) father. There is an obvious tension between Delia and her mother and this tension finds its ultimate expression in the conflict between the mother's wish to move to Kilkenny and open a dressmaker's shop and Delia's desire to grow up in the rural environment of County Kildare.

Virago Modern Classics

Maura Laverty

Never No More

The problem is resolved by Gran, who offers to keep Delia with her and use the few shillings she has 'between herself and the Union' to pay for her granddaughter's education. From then on, Gran becomes the centre of the book.

> Oh Gran! Was there ever anyone like you? There she sat, like a little withered apple of a woman. For all her sixty-eight years, her back beneath the black cloth bodice was as straight as a sergeant major's. She was unloved by the slovenly and malicious and foolish. They resented her neat briskness, her wide charity, her impatience with fools. Such souls apart, everyone else in Ballyderrig loved her.

Delia's life in Derrymore House, Gran's snug farmhouse two miles outside Ballyderrig, begins that very night and the rest of the book describes the almost idyllic rural life she lived there for the next two years and beyond. The author's skill is so subtle that the narration never slips into sentimentality. There is an almost boundless toleration for life's aberrations within the community which expresses itself in a warm and generous humanity tinged with a natural but deep spirituality.

Indeed the atmosphere of the book is so wholesome that reading it is like having your hands in a bowl of flour. All human crises can be soothed by a special recipe and all human aberrations are but a wee slip that can be rectified by a good solid home-cooked meal.

Scothscéalta

PÁDRAIC Ó CONAIRE

Tá scéal i mbéaloideas an teaghlaigh seo againne go mbíodh nós ag Pádraic Ó Conaire bualadh isteach chuig ár seanathair, Tom 'Cork' Kenny, a bhí ina eagarthóir ar an *Connacht Tribune*, nuair a bhíodh easpa airgid air – rud a tharlaíodh minic go leor. Chuireadh mo sheanathair an scríbhneoir ina shuí ag bord i seomra faoi leith agus thugadh sé peann agus páipéar dó. Ansin chuireadh sé an seomra faoi ghlas. Ní osclaíodh sé an doras nó go gcuirfeadh an Conaireach gearrscéal críochnaithe amach faoi bhun an dorais. Ansin, agus ní go dtí sin, thugadh ár seanathair an t-airgead dó.

Rugadh Pádraic Ó Conaire i nGaillimh sa bhliain 1882. Thréig a athair an teaghlach in 1888 agus d'éag a mháthair in 1893. Chuaigh an Conaireach óg chun cónaithe lena uncail i Ros Muc, áit ar fhoghlaim sé a chuid Gaeilge. D'fhreastail sé ar Choláiste Rockwell agus ar Choláiste na Carraige Duibhe ina dhiaidh sin. Ansin chuaigh sé go Londain sa bhliain 1899. Phós sé i 1903 agus bhí ceathrar clainne aige. Thosaigh sé ag scríobh ag an am seo agus bhuaigh sé cuid mhaith duaiseanna ag an Oireachtas. Thosaigh sé ag ól go trom, áfach, agus d'fhill sé ar Éirinn i 1914 agus chaith sé an chuid eile dá shaol ar an mbóthar ag saothrú cibé airgead a d'fhéadfadh sé lena chuid scríbhneoireachta. Fuair sé bás agus é beo bocht in Ospidéal an Richmond i mBaile Átha Cliath i 1929.

B'fhéidir gurbh fhear siúlach é Pádraic Ó Conaire ach ba dhroichead riachtanach é idir seantraidisiún liteartha na Gaeilge

agus litríocht nua-aimseartha na hEorpa.

Is óna pheann a tháinig cuid de na sleachta is cáiliúla i litríocht na Gaeilge, an sliocht seo a leanas ina measc: 'I gCinn Mhara bhíos nuair a chuireas aithne ar m'asal beag dubh i dtosach. Lá aonaigh a bhí ann, agus bhí sé ina sheasamh ansin cois claí agus a thóin le gaoth, gan aird aige ar an saol ná ag an saol air.' An deacracht is mó a bhaineann le cur amach liteartha an Chonairigh, go bhfuil sé scaipthe. Tar éis a bháis i 1928, ní raibh cnuasach ceart dá chuid gearrscéalta le fáil go dtí gur foilsíodh an cnuasach a chuir Tomás de Bhaldraithe amach i 1956 faoin teideal *Scothscéalta*.

Tá an cnuasach seo ag cur thar maoil le samplaí saibhre den stíl lom, díreach a bhí ag an gConaireach, stíl nach facthas i litríocht na Gaeilge go dtí sin. Tosaíonn an gearrscéal 'Anam an Easpaig' leis an alt seo a leanas:

> Bhí an t-easpag ina chodladh. Ní raibh le feiceáil ach a shrón, a bhéal, a smig agus leathshúil leis nuair a d'fhéach an fear aimsire, tiománaí an ghluaisteáin, isteach trí na fuinneoga air. Bhí faoi inseacht dó go gcaithfeadh sé moill a chur air, go raibh rud éigin ar cearr le inneall an chairr, ach nuair a thug sé faoi deara sa gcúinne é, agus a raibh de chótaí móra agus eile bhí aige timpeall air, shíl sé go mb'fhearr dhó féin gan bacadh leis go gcuirfeadh sé caoi ar an inneall diabhalta sin gan mhaith.

Titeann an stíl seo próis go héasca, ceolmhar ar na cluasa. Tá sé bríomhar, díreach agus músclaítear suim an léitheora ar an bpointe. Mealltar isteach sa scéal é agus tá an seanchas chomh maith sin ag Pádraic Ó Conaire go bhfanann sé leis go dtí an focal deireanach. Fiú mura bhfuil Gaeilge mhaith ag an léitheoir, bainfidh sé sult as na gearrscéalta seo.

The Course of Irish History

EDITED BY T.W. MOODY AND F.X. MARTIN

Some years ago – when pedestrianisation of Galway was still in the future, as was the general use of credit cards – a rather elderly American visited the shop. He was looking for a one-volume balanced history of Ireland, not an easy book to find. After some tentative suggestions, P.W. Joyce's *History of Ireland* was selected. The bill came to nine pounds, nine and sixpence, or about twelve dollars.

To his horror, the man discovered he had no cash.

'No problem,' said Thomas, 'We'll be happy to take your personal cheque in dollars.'

'But you don't know me.'

'That doesn't matter. Your cheque is most acceptable to us.'

The man was still reluctant to accept this solution and an argument ensued, becoming livelier and livelier until Thomas finally insisted, 'For God's sake man, give us the damned thing. You are not going to bounce a twelve-dollar cheque.'

The man relented, took out his cheque book, made a cheque out to Kenny's for twelve dollars. He then signed it William Randolph Hearst. Thomas looked at him.

'I don't believe this. You could buy the whole street, but you were afraid to sign a twelve-dollar cheque.'

'This wouldn't have happened me in the States,' came the simple reply.

A lively conversation followed and both men repaired to Tigh Neachtain, a local hostelry where, to celebrate this extraordinary

THE COURSE
OF
IRISH HISTORY

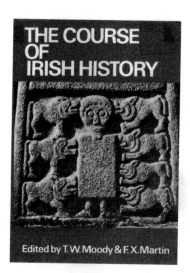

Edited by T. W. Moody & F. X. Martin

event, William Randolph Hearst borrowed twenty pounds from my brother to buy a round.

Six weeks later, the first request came to us from abroad for a copy of P.W. Joyce's *History of Ireland*. Then, with many other requests came the press snippets: on his return to the States Hearst had written and syndicated an editorial – right across the USA – talking about a bookshop in Galway and the wonderful history of Ireland he had got there. It took us nearly two and a half years to fill the order as, sadly, the book was out of print. Sadder still, we cashed the cheque.

Had this happened a couple of years later and *The Course of Irish History* been in print, the orders would have been filled immediately. Edited by two of Ireland's most prominent historians F. X. Martin and T. W. Moody the book was first published by Mercier Press in 1967. There have since been four revised and enlarged editions and it has been reprinted at least fifty times.

The Course of Irish History was originally a pioneering television documentary of twenty-one programmes broadcast by RTÉ in 1966 as part of the fiftieth anniversary celebrations of the 1916 Rising. As Moody and Martin wrote in the first preface of the book: 'The aim of the series was to present a survey of Irish history that would be both popular and authoritative, concise but comprehensive, highly selective while at the same time balanced and fair-minded, critical but constructive and sympathetic.'

The edition to hand has twenty-four chapters, each written by a prominent historian covering different aspects of Irish history. The reader can visit an era of particular interest or explore the history of Ireland from its beginnings to the end of the twentieth century. In terms of an objective one-volume history of Ireland, there are few, if any, general histories that compare with it. *The Course of Irish History* is a cornerstone of any Irish library.

The Turf-cutter's Donkey

Patricia Lynch

Born in Cork in 1898, Patricia Lynch went to live in London after her father died. After finishing her formal education in England, Scotland and Belgium, she became a journalist and an activist in the woman's movement: She was sent to cover the 1916 Rising by Sylvia Pankhurst and her report, published in *Worker's Dreadnought*, was the first sympathetic account of the Rising to be published in England. She settled in Dublin in 1920 and married the socialist writer R. M. Fox.

Beginning with *The Turf-cutter's Donkey* published in 1935, she became a prolific and world-famous children's writer, creating many delightful characters such as Brogeen the Leprechaun and Long Ears. She died in 1972.

Opening the cover of Patricia Lynch's *The Turf-cutter's Donkey* is like slipping on a magical cloak: immediately you are in a world of imagination where everything – no matter how fantastic – is normal.

From the first sentence, the reader is introduced to Eileen and Seamus, the turf-cutter's children, who live in a cabin just beyond the crossroads at the edge of the great bog. Their father, we are told, 'knew so many songs to sing and so many tunes to whistle that he hadn't a great deal of time for turf cutting.' Their mother was a lace-maker who sold her lace 'on fair day at the town on the other side of Flat Top Mountain.'

They had Big Fella the dog and Rose the cat, 'a grand little red

The
Turf-cutter's
Donkey

PATRICIA LYNCH

Illustrations by Jack B. Yeats

cow from Kerry, an elegant pink pig in a neat, tidy sty, when the creature would stay there, and any number of hens and chickens, so they didn't do too badly.'

It all starts with Eileen's wish for a donkey, her sore toe and 'the battered silver teapot, no bigger than a breakfast cup.' Suddenly, the little grey donkey of Eileen's dreams appears, along with many more characters: tinkers (especially the King) and the Water Rat who likes washing his whiskers.

Pure, innocent magic.

All of this leads to a series of wonderful adventures beginning with the magic pool at the top of Flat Top Mountain. Time means nothing, logic doesn't exist. The reader, enchanted by a magnificently energetic text, is transported on a river of fanciful adventure.

We travel back in time with ease. We meet Fionn Mac Cumhail, the Dé Danann and the Fir Bolg and greet them as old friends. There is a complete suspension of disbelief and the reader participates with enthusiasm.

The Turf-cutter's Donkey is an unsung children's classic. Uncluttered, uncomplicated and magical, it is a triumph of the imagination.

Captain Boycott

PHILIP ROONEY

A misconception of mine, held for years, was that Philip Rooney hailed from County Down and that there was a vague relationship between him and Dan Rooney of the Pittsburgh Steelers. A quick look at the author's biographical blurbs – he is a native of Collooney, County Sligo – would have quickly put that misconception to rights, but reference to it here allows me an opportunity to pay tribute to the largely unsung contribution made by the Rooney of Pittsburgh to Irish literature.

For over twenty-five years now, the Rooney Prize has given a lifeline to one young writer a year to continue writing. The fund was inaugurated at a time when such prizes were almost non-existent and because it is awarded for a first published work, it has given vital support to writers at the point in their careers where they are most vulnerable. Many of the established writers working in Ireland today owe the Rooney family a debt of gratitude.

It is a curious coincidence that much in the same way as the Rooney Prize has been overshadowed by other literary prizes, Philip Rooney's work has been ignored by contemporary commentators. He does not feature in *The Oxford Companion to Irish Literature* or in *The Encyclopaedia of Ireland*. He has been largely forgotten, but in his day he was considered one of the leading figures among the more popular Irish novelists of the 1940s and 1950s. *Captain Boycott*, first published in 1946, was his most successful and best book.

PHILIP ROONEY'S

CAPTAIN BOYCOTT

THE MAN WHOSE NAME GAVE
A DREADED WORD TO THE ENGLISH
LANGUAGE IN THE STORMY DAYS
OF THE LAND LEAGUE

ANVIL BOOKS

3/6

Philip Rooney was born in 1907 and educated in Limerick. He worked as a bank clerk in the midlands before illness forced him to retire. He began to write short stories and one of them won a prize in a Hospital Sweeps competition. His first novel *All Out to Win* was published in 1935. He worked as a journalist and broadcaster. In 1953, he became Head of Scriptwriting in Radio Éireann, transferring to television in 1961. He died suddenly in Dublin in 1962.

Captain Boycott is a historical romance. There is the landlord's agent trying to extract every penny in rent out of his tenants. The tenants are starving, unable to pay the rents and facing eviction. In between these two extremes is a whole panorama of characters all playing their roles with zest. At the heart of the book is the love story between Hugh Davin, the schoolteacher and would-be rebel, and Anne Killian, whose father, a tenant, threatens to pull himself out of poverty, thereby earning himself the hatred of his peers.

Rooney's strength as a novelist is that he avoids stereotyping his characters and weaves a wonderful tale of love and intrigue where the social barriers are often blurred and the characters are victims of events far beyond their own control.

As well as telling the story of Captain Boycott and the Land War in the Mayo of the 1880s, the novel also contains some wonderful individual vignettes, especially of the people living in the Big House. The characters of Watty Connell, the process server, and Captain Boycott's mother are skilfully drawn.

Although published in the 1940s, *Captain Boycott* seems as fresh now as it did then. It is a book to curl up with.

Nineteen Acres

John Healy

Just after two in the afternoon you'd see them come up the town. They were easily recognisable. Heads down, caps pulled over the eyes, carrying their belongings in a cardboard case tied with a handy piece of string, they walked with resignation towards the boat train. The townspeople ignored them, for they were tangible proof that the much-vaunted society we all lived in was a failure. They were the emigrants and in 1950s and early 1960s Ireland they were an everyday reality.

In the late 1970s, Father handed me a manuscript and said, 'Read that.' Anne and I had just married. We were living in a small basement flat at the back of a house on Threadneedle Road. Money was tight and, although I had started to work in the bookshop, Anne was the wage earner and kept our confidence high. I took the manuscript home and read it in a couple of hours. My belief in following a career as a bookseller was revitalised with a vengeance. This was a classic and we were going to publish it. The title was *Nineteen Acres* and its author was John Healy.

Born in Charlestown County Mayo in 1930, John Healy was to be a leading Irish political journalist and broadcaster for more than three decades, especially during the fifteen years he wrote the 'Backbencher' column for *The Irish Times*.

Healy's book, *Death of an Irish Town*, published in 1968, exposed the destruction of the social and cultural fabric in the West of Ireland – specifically in his home town of Charlestown

– ignored by uncaring bureaucracies in Dublin. It became a journalistic classic. John Healy died in 1991.

'Keep your mouth and your legs closed. Keep your ears open. And send home the ticket for Anne.' How many thousands of tearful heartbroken mothers gave this advice to daughters they would never see again. Here the daughter in question was to become the author's mother for she was one of the lucky ones who returned.

Initially, *Nineteen Acres* is a straigfhtforward recounting of Healy's own upbringing but, as the narration develops, we're given the real story: the life of his mother and her various siblings and their experience of life in America. As he probes deeper, Healy discovers that the romantic perception of life in the USA was far from the truth and the personal sacrifices made by the emigrants to maintain the status quo of the American letter or parcel were often personally impoverishing. As time takes its toll in Mayo and a generation passes on, Healy finally uncovers the vital force that kept these emigrants going and here we reach the real heart of the book and its emotive strength.

John Healy's *Nineteen Acres* is one of the few books that recognises the contribution to Irish life made by hundreds of thousands of Irish emigrants and the extraordinary personal sacrifices they made to do this. It recognises also the loneliness they suffered – and the ingratitude of an uncaring society back home.

Langrishe Go Down

AIDAN HIGGINS

Aidan Higgins is one of the great enigmas of modern Irish literature. He belongs to an almost underground stratum of Irish writers whose works, published to great critical acclaim, attract little popular reaction. However, these writers (other examples include Forrest Reid and James Hanley) have a rich and extensive output and represent the hidden treasures of the Irish literary canon.

Set in the author's home county of Kildare, *Langrishe Go Down* is ostensibly about the final demise of the 'Big House' but under Higgins's skilful pen, it becomes much more than that.

Aidan Higgins was born in 1927 in Celbridge, County Kildare, to a former land-owning family. After finishing his formal education in Clongowes Wood, he lived in South Africa, Germany, London, Southern Spain and Ireland. His first book, a collection of short stories entitled *Felo Da Se*, was published in 1960 and since then there have been a number of autobiographical works and novels, the best known being *Langrishe Go Down*, first published in 1966.

The book begins with an uncanny evocation of a bus journey from Dublin to Kildare in the 1930s. Helen Langrishe is going home to her sisters but there is a sense of doom about the journey.

While the central figures of the book are the four spinster sisters and its theme is their increasing isolation, the depth of this isolation is best epitomised by Higgins in his vignette of their

father's pathetic attempt to introduce new farming methods to his labourers:

> Grouped around him, they were listening open-mouthed. He spoke rapidly in his thin voice, striking his thigh with a switch for emphasis, pulling the ends of his waistcoat down, shooting his cuffs, studying their inscrutable faces. Yis sur, yis sur. When he became excited, his voice grew reedier: a voice sharp and high-toned – disagreeable. The men did not believe in his new-fangled notions, not even they could follow them. He began waving his hands then, powerless to improve or change anything – loose at the wrists, the gesture that scatters fowl. 'Well, to work men! To work! I think we understand each other now. We have wasted too much time talking.' Their inscrutable faces. Yis sur, yis sur.

The wonderful ironic humour employed in this scene appears from time to time throughout the book, but the sense of impending doom prevails. Even the brief love affair between Helen and the German Otto fails to lift the gloom, and the book ends in the inevitable demise of the Langrishe household which is cleverly contrasted, through the use of contemporary newspapers, with the final death throes of the Hapsburg Empire.

The Visitor

MAEVE BRENNAN

Maeve Brennan's father participated in the 1916 Easter Rising and was sentenced to death, a sentence later commuted to penal servitude. On his release, he continued to be politically active and was in prison when Maeve was born in 1917. The family moved to Washington in 1934 when her father was appointed Irish Ambassador to the US. When they returned to Ireland in 1944, Maeve moved to New York where she worked as a journalist for *Harper's Bazaar*. In 1949 she became a staff writer with the *New Yorker*, where she was celebrated for her short stories. She was always eccentric; her mental health deteriorated and she was hospitalised on a number of occasions. She died destitute in 1993. *The Visitor* was written in the 1940s but not published until 2000, after the only known copy of the manuscript was discovered in a university archive.

At the beginning of *The Visitor* Anastasia King, a young lady, is returning to Dublin after six years in Paris. There is an immediate sense of foreboding. As the cab leaves the station, we are told that: 'Anastasia slumped lower in her seat trying not to recognise the sudden melancholy that was on her. The cabman drove without a word and his silence seemed sullen. She felt rebuffed for no reason.'

She is returning to her grandmother's house which is at once familiar and forbidding. Brennan is relentless in the bleak build-up, and the first description of the grandmother, who has been

MAEVE BRENNAN

'An astonishing miniature masterpiece'
NUALA O'FAOLAIN

THE VISITOR

waiting for Anastasia, is unparalleled as a portrait of restrained and calculated cruelty:

> She kissed her grandmother hastily, avoiding her eyes. The grandmother did not move from the door of the sitting room. She stood in the doorway, having just got up from the fireside and her reading, and contemplated Anastasia and Anastasia's luggage crowding the hall. She was still the same, with her delicate and ruminative and ladylike face and her hands clasped in front of her. Anastasia thought, she is waiting for me to make some mistake.

With consummate skill, Brennan develops the tension between Anastasia and her grandmother. There are two other characters in the novella, not to provide some relief, as might be expected, but to accentuate and reinforce the darkness. Any glimmer of hope is quickly snuffed out.

Katharine, the grandmother's maid, is imprisoned by the longevity of her domestic service. Any attempts to make Anastasia welcome in the house are severely dealt with by the grandmother, and Katharine's subservient position and loneliness are confirmed.

The only other character in the novella is Miss Kilbride, a family friend who lives alone. Once, she was in love but her bedridden mother would not let her marry and her fate was sealed. As a final act of defiance, on her deathbed Miss Kilbride sets Anastasia a task. It is this request that ignites the inevitable confrontation between Anastasia and her grandmother, and a finale that leaves the reader gasping.

The Year of Liberty

Thomas Pakenham

Too often, history books are couched in a language that is beyond the reach of the general reading public and, to a large extent, the average man in the street remains uninformed. Fortunately, from time to time, a book does surface that appeals to a wider audience, keeps the flame of knowledge alive and is an invaluable addition to our own sense of who we are. Thomas Pakenham's *The Year of Liberty*, first published in 1970, is one such book.

The son of Frank Pakenham, the Earl of Longford, and Elizabeth Longford, Thomas Pakenham comes from a family of writers. He was educated at Oxford and spent a year wandering through Ethiopia and the Middle East. For five years he worked as a journalist in London, where he became educational correspondent for the *Observer*. In the mid sixties, he moved to Ireland and spent five years researching and writing *The Year of Liberty*.

Pakenham's approach is direct. There is no lengthy overview of the origins of the 1798 Rebellion or in-depth analysis of the political, social or economic conditions that gave rise to it. There is on the contrary a sense of Pakenham rolling up his sleeves and getting stuck into it. The first three paragraphs of the preface read:

> The Rebellion of 1798 is the most violent and tragic event in Irish history between the Jacobite wars and the Great Famine.

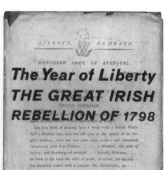

In the space of a few weeks, 30,000 people – peasants armed with pikes and pitchforks, defenceless women and children – were cut down or shot or blown like chaff as they charged up to the mouth of the cannon.

The results of the Rebellion were no less disastrous: Britain imposed a Union on terms that proved unacceptable to the majority of the Irish people, and there was a legacy of violence and hatred that has persisted to the present day.

This direct style continues right through the book. There is a brief preamble describing the failed Bantry Bay invasion by the French fleet in 1796 and the events of the months leading up to the Rising, but the bulk of the book deals with the actual Rebellion itself, using a diary format.

While there may be some confusion from time to time, the overall effect is refreshing, enthralling and informative. The reader has a wonderful sense of the ebb and flow of the conflict as well as its immediacy. Battles were won and lost by quickly-taken decisions. Thousands were killed. Sometimes people were executed on a whim. Atrocities were commonplace.

Above all *The Year of Liberty* informs us of the conflagration that gave rise to modern Irish society, its political, social and religious ethos, and, as such, is essential reading for anyone interested in modern Irish history.

The Hounds of the Morrigan

Pat O'Shea

Within minutes of meeting Pat O'Shea you felt as if you had known her all your life. She was a naturally benevolent and kind lady: you knew your innermost thoughts, secrets and aspirations would always receive a sympathetic hearing from her and, no matter what happened, she was always there with the pot of tea and plate of scones by the fireside – smiling, encouraging, welcoming, loving.

Paradoxically, there was an almost childlike innocence about her that was infectious. In the early days of the Galway Arts Festival she was standing outside the shop watching a Macnas parade pass down High Street. She laughed, cried, shrieked, clapped her hands, jumped for joy, yahooed, yelled, shouted encouragement, derided to such an extent that a person had a right to be confused as to whether she was a respectable lady of advanced years or a wide-eyed young child looking at her first parade.

Somehow, it came as no surprise to us when Pat announced that she had just had a book published and that it was a children's book. However, when she told us that it was published by Oxford University Press, we sat up and took notice. And when we finally got the book, we weren't disappointed. *The Hounds of the Morrigan* is a rare gem and a terrific read.

The book is set in Galway, where Pat O'Shea was born in 1931 (she left it for Manchester in 1947, where she lived until her death in 2007). The theme of the book is the traditional battle between

good and evil. Pidge (Patrick Joseph or PJ) finds himself outside St Nicholas's Church with some hours to spare. His feet take him down High Street and he wanders into a second-hand bookshop where the grumpy old bookseller ignores him. (The bookshop is purportedly Kenny's, 'the bookshop of my childhood,' but of course it couldn't be: there were never any grumpy old booksellers in Kenny's.)

Pidge wanders into the back of the shop where he picks up some pages loosely kept together. A title page tells him it is a *Book of Patrick's Writings*, but in this book, nothing is what it appears to be, and immediately the fun starts and the magic begins.

As the story develops, O'Shea's imagination runs wild. We discover that these pages discovered by Pidge hold an evil spirit, the Olc Glass, and if the Morrigan, the Goddess of Evil, can manage to release this spirit a terrible destruction will ravage the land. Flanked by her pack of sinister hounds, she roams the countryside and her magic is all-powerful.

The finding of the manuscript sends Pidge and his little sister Bridget – who thinks the whole thing is great fun – on a long and mysterious journey to an unknown destination. Their task is to prevent the Morrigan from gaining possession of the Olc Glass. They are constantly shadowed by the hounds who are ready to attack at every instant, but the Dodge, the Goddess of All Things Good, has chosen Pidge to outwit the Goddess of Evil.

The result is a book of unadulterated magic and fantasy, a story told with a delightful sense of fun and laughter.

Islanders

PEADAR O'DONNELL

'That book wrote itself.'

These words were spoken quietly by the old man sitting in the chair, so quietly they were nearly missed. Somebody had just handed him a first edition of the book and his reaction had been reflective, almost nostalgic. Fortunately, his words were picked up and the obvious question, 'How?' was asked.

'When I was in solitary confinement, there was nothing in the cell. Even the light was poor. To keep my sanity, I began to compose this book in my head. As soon as they let me out, I asked for pencil and paper, sat down and wrote it from start to finish in one straight draft.'

Normally, such a statement would be taken with a pinch of salt, but when the person talking is Peadar O'Donnell, there is no doubting its veracity.

Born in Meenmore, County Donegal, in 1893, Peadar O'Donnell initially trained as a teacher and became school principal on Arranmore. Horrified by the grinding poverty on the island and by the conditions suffered by its migrant workers, he became a union organiser.

He fought on the Republican side of the Civil War and received a two-year prison sentence, part of which he spent in solitary confinement. After his release he edited two Republican newspapers *An t-Óglach* and *An Phoblacht*, led agitation against the land annuities, founded the Republican Congress in 1934

and recruited for the International Brigade during the Spanish Civil War.

He co-founded, with Sean O'Faolain, the seminal Irish review *The Bell* in October 1940, a date that marks the beginning of the real Irish Literary Renaissance. It is a curious fact that the doors of our shop opened exactly one month later, on 29 November 1940. O'Donnell wrote several memoirs and novels, his last being *Proud Island,* published in 1975. He spent his final years campaigning for nuclear disarmament and for improved conditions in the West of Ireland. He died in 1986, aged ninety-three.

First published in 1927, *Islanders* (the book handed to him that day in the shop) is deceptively simple. The Doogan family are eking out existence on an island off the Donegal coast. Their poverty is such that the acquisition of two bucketfuls of winkles is seen as a considerable addition to the wealth of the home and a cause for celebration.

Despite its short length, the panorama of the book is heroic, not to say epic. By focusing on the one family, especially the mother Mary and son Charlie, O'Donnell manages to distil the humanity of the Islanders and their tragic pathos. Not a word is wasted. The concision of language is one of the book's remarkable achievements.

Through the power of O'Donnell's narration the history of the Doogan family transcends the island. The conditions in which they live, the humanity they aspire to, their inevitable tragic fate – all mirror the state of Ireland at the time.

The Voyage of St Brendan

John J. O'Meara

When John McGahern formally opened our refurbished shop in 1996, he spoke about the intimacy of reading. Nothing, he said, could be more private or more relaxing than the act of reading. Nobody can disturb or discern what is happening between the reader and the page. It is the ultimate intimate moment.

In a memoir of the Galway Blazers which we published in 1988, the author, Brigadier Edmund Mahoney, pauses a moment from his pursuit of the wily fox to ponder the ancient ruins that dot the countryside. It does no harm, he writes, to lean against these old walls now and again, and contemplate their erstwhile occupants and the lives they led.

Curiously, John J. O'Meara's translation of *Navigatio Sancti Brendani Abbatis* under the title *The Voyage of Saint Brendan: Journey to the Promised Land* brings these two seemingly disparate facts into focus.

Saint Brendan represents all that is adventurous in the Irish psyche, but his achievements are seen through somewhat hazy glasses. The possibility that he may have sailed as far as present-day America strikes a deep chord in today's Ireland, which claims to have at least one representative in every corner of the globe.

John Joseph O'Meara was born in Eyrecour,t County Galway, in 1915. Educated in Cashel and University College Dublin, he went on to complete a doctorate in classics in Oxford. He was appointed Professor of Latin in University College Dublin

in 1948. He wrote several books relating to the later classics, more especially on St Augustine. He also published a book on Eriugena, the early-Christian Irish philosopher, and a translation of Giraldus Cambrensis's *Topography of Ireland*, an unflattering account of a trip to Ireland by the 12th-century priest Gerald de Barri. In later years he wrote an autobiographical account of his youth in Eyrecourt and a collection of short stories set there.

This translation, first published in 1976, allows us the opportunity to get as close as we can to the realities of St Brendan and his voyages. To do this, however, we must prepare ourselves, and O'Meara's excellent introduction to the text goes a long way in assisting us.

He underlines the spirit of the times when Brendan lived and notes that, within a hundred years of his death, a written account of his voyage was probably extant. The source for the present translation was written in Ireland 'perhaps as early as 800'. He stresses the fact that early Irish monasticism is the 'firm basis of reality in the story of Brendan's voyage'.

The book's first paragraph reads:

> Saint Brendan, son of Findlug, descendant of Alte, was born among the Eoganacht of Loch Léin in the land of the men of Munster. He was a man of great abstinence, famous for his mighty works and father of nearly three thousand monks.

Soon we find ourselves immersed in a wonderful story of the eternal Christian pilgrimage to the Promised Land, with an Irish twist or two. The language is deceptively simple but it is useful to try and approach it as the people of the day would have read or heard it. Then it takes on a deeper meaning which greatly enhances it and enriches our experience of reading it.

The Weaver's Grave

SEUMAS O'KELLY

A curiosity of the book world is just how unavailable copies of recognised classics can be. Books in Ireland tend to have a short shelf life. Print runs are small and once an edition is sold out it can be years before it is reprinted. In the case of Seumas O'Kelly's *The Weaver's Grave*, I knew that Norman Morgan, the Loughrea bibliographer, not only would have a copy, but he would have it in a first edition.

I was right. Being the bookman he is, his copy had further local connotations.

'Do you recognise the writing?' he asked, handing me the scored copy.

'An tAthair Eric,' I said, immediately awash with memories. An tAthair Eric McFhinn was possibly the greatest collector of Irish-language books in the west of Ireland.

One afternoon, in the early 1960s, having just published his first Irish-language catalogue, Father was standing inside the front door of the shop. An t-Athair Eric walked in. Father handed him a catalogue and directed him to the Irish language section. About twenty minutes later, an t-Athair Eric walked out without buying a book. Father was disgusted. The following day, the catalogue arrived back in the afternoon post with orders for over one third of its content.

The author Seumas O'Kelly was born near Loughrea, County Galway about 1875. Although having little or no formal

education, he became a prominent journalist in nationalist circles. He joined The *Southern Star* in 1903 and rose to edit it and several other newspaper titles. Many of his plays were produced in the Abbey and he also published a number of novels and short-story collections, all set in the rural Ireland of his youth. He died of a heart attack during a raid on the Sinn Féin offices three days after the Armistice of 11 November 1918.

The Weaver's Grave, published in 1912, is O'Kelly's masterpiece. Mortimer Hehir, the weaver, has died. His grave is the last plot in Cloon Na Marv, but it is so long since anyone has been buried there that no one knows its exact location.

The narration opens with Meehaul Lyskey the nail maker, Cahir Bowes the stone breaker, the grave-digger twins and the widow of the weaver crossing the stile into the graveyard. Being called upon to fulfil the important task of finding the weaver's grave gives Meehaul and Cahir, two old men, a new lease of life. Their initial failure to do this causes all the old antagonisms to surface.

Gradually, however, and with tremendous skill, O'Kelly shifts the emphasis away from the two old men, through the grave-diggers, to the widow who quietly asserts her own individuality and wakens to a new love, shrugging off the encroaching senility of her immediate surroundings.

The Weaver's Grave, with its strong satire, acerbic sense of humour and tremendous insight into the rural life of western Ireland at the beginning of the twentieth century, is a minor classic.

The Untilled Field

George Moore

During my student days in Paris, Mother came to visit and stayed in a hotel opposite La Gare du Nord. She had read previously that George Moore had stayed in the same area. As far as she was concerned it was in the same hotel. Part of our daily ritual was to have afternoon coffee in the adjacent café as, she insisted, George Moore would have done.

Despite the indifference of the multitudinous Parisians who passed us that week, the import of that little literary celebration remains as strong to me now as it did then. La Gare du Nord never ceases to conjure up an image of late-nineteenth-century Paris, a group of men, curiously no women, in smoking jackets with cigars, petits fours and cups of coffee discussing some aesthetic point of literature, among them Emile Zola and George Moore.

Nowadays, Moore has something of a quixotic image. Born in County Mayo in 1852, the son of a Catholic landlord, he was sent to England at the age of nine to be educated. At fifteen, he was sent home, a hopeless case. His father died in 1870, leaving him an estate of 12,000 acres. Three years later he went to Paris to study art, but failed as an artist and was beginning to establish himself as a writer when he was called home because of the Land War.

Appointing a land agent to administer the Mayo estate, he left for London to continue his literary career. Attracted by W.B. Yeats to the fledgling Irish Literary Theatre, he collaborated in several plays produced there, more especially those written by

Edward Martyn, also a Catholic landlord. He moved to Dublin in 1901. *The Untilled Field* was first published in 1903.

Moore was avowedly anti-clerical, certainly later in his career, and an absentee landlord – yet the stories in this collection demonstrate a warm empathy towards the peasantry of the west of Ireland and towards the clergy who minister to them.

This is certainly evident in 'The Exile', the opening story, in which the protagonists, lay and clerical, find themselves faced with an unusual situation, which is resolved in a most pragmatic manner. Despite the biting satire and sardonic humour which permeate the story, all the characters have a deep humanity and compassion. The fact that nobody loses face and everyone maintains a sense of dignity underlines the success of the story.

'The Exile' is followed by the classic story 'Home-Sickness', in which the same sense of humanity prevails. It has strong autobiographical undertones.

There follows a panorama of characters, nearly all from the same community in Mayo. The collection could be compared to several modern-day soap operas. The inspirations, foibles, strengths and weaknesses of the community are laid before us, without comment. There is, however, a laconic humour present – most especially in the title story – which adds a wonderful sense of irony to the collection, making it one of the great classics of Irish literature.

Blackcock's Feather

MAURICE WALSH

This is the story of me, David Gordon, and I will begin
on that day in May that I walked down the quay-wall
at Mouth of Avon, below Bristol, and held discourse
with one Diggory, sailing master of the *Speckled Hind*. I
begin on that day because it was on that day life began
for me.

One of the great tragedies of modern technology, not to
mention modern education, is that there is at least one generation
of Irish people who have never had the pleasure of opening a
book and reading a first paragraph as powerful and as promising
as that of Maurice Walsh's *Blackcock's Feather*.

Maurice Walsh was born near Listowel, County Kerry in 1879,
and was educated locally. In 1901, he entered the Customs and
Excise Service and spent twenty years in the Scottish Highlands,
where it is said he acquired a connoisseur's taste for whiskey. In
1922, he transferred to the Irish service and returned to Ireland.

His first novel, *A Key Above the Door*, was published in 1926
and he rapidly became one of the most popular writers in
Ireland, England and America, writing a series of romances set in
Scotland and the west of Ireland over the next thirty-odd years.
His story *The Quiet Man* is said to be the source for the classic
John Houston film of the same name, although it is also claimed

that his novel *Green Rushes* was the inspiration.

Blackcock's Feather was published in 1932 and within a decade there were few Irish households that didn't have a copy. The story begins, as we have just read, in Mouth of Avon just below Bristol, but after some sparkling swordsmanship and an uncomfortable voyage we are walking the streets of a Gaelic-speaking Tudor Dublin. Hugh O'Neill and Red Hugh O'Donnell have defeated the English in a number of battles, notably Clontibret, and the streets are alive with soldiers, rumour and suspicion.

We move from Dublin to Dungiven and, after a wee diversion, to south Galway to snatch a willing bride from an unwilling father, then, after an enforced fishing holiday on Lough Corrib, to Hugh O'Neill's stronghold in Dungannon. Here, at last, there is a slight pause before we join up with O'Donnell's forces to repel an English attempt at incursion into the North, and the story ends up with the battle of Athenry and on the shores of the Corrib.

This an unputdownable book. They simply don't write them like this any more. It is a microcosm of life in Ireland at the end of the Tudor era; a pen-picture of a soldier's life during those heady days when the hope for Ireland's cause was strong. It also hints at the underlying suffering of the 'mere' Irish under Elizabeth's rule.

Maurice Walsh's powerful narrative is an example of Irish storytelling at its best. A book to be enjoyed by all ages, *Blackcock's Feather* could well be one of the best Irish historical romances ever written.

Remembering Ahanagran

RICHARD WHITE

When *Remembering Ahanagran* was first published in 1996, its author was the Professor of Modern History at Stanford University, California. His father was born in Boston of Russian-Jewish ancestry. His mother was from the townland of Ahanagran in North Kerry.

The starting point of the book is a house fire in Ahanagran in January 1995. Although the occupants of the burning house were unharmed, the ramifications of the fire were huge. It was in the light of that burning house, White tells us, that he could hope to understand the cultural identity he had inherited from his mother.

To do this, he takes us back to his mother's (her name was Sara Walsh) childhood in Ahanagran and more specifically to 1936 when, at the age of sixteen, she travelled on her own from her north Kerry home to Chicago, her father having sent for her. There she found her family living in something of a Chicago-Irish ghetto. The household was crippled by a high level of alcoholism and there was little hope of social or economic advancement.

Sara was resourceful and managed to get a job in the Chicago Municipal Airport. This job proved to be her ticket out of the ghetto and it was also through it that she met her husband-to-be, Harry White.

Sara brought with her to America a head full of stories and memories. Among these was a vivid memory of a Black-and-Tan

raid on their home in Ahanagran, during which her mother was physically assaulted.

These stories were part of Richard White's childhood and he took them at face value. Later on, however, as a professional historian, he searched the official sources for evidence that this raid, amongst other events, actually took place. But he could find none.

The book is an attempt to explore the veracity of his mother's recollections. He tells us he wants to 'interrogate' them out of respect for her but he also wants to discover what they represent in the America of today. He comes to realise that 'beneath these personal stories simmers our ongoing contest over what America is and who defines it.' He sees this contest as being central to his mother's life and to American history. He continues:

> Immigration is not always about leaving a part behind, but neither is it simply the transportation of culture and traditions from one place to another. American is not something a person learns to be, it is an identity contested and fought over. Boundaries do not create identities, boundaries are permeable. There is no category that can embrace even one of us, we are all many people.

Remembering Ahanagran is a fascinating read. White's prose is clear and honest. Coupled with his intellectual curiosity, there is a strong narrative and human quality in the book that gives it integrity and makes it accessible to a wide audience. It is one of the great unsung classics of Irish emigration.

The Dark

John McGahern

With the publication of *The Dark* John McGahern came of literary age, as did Ireland. It was one of the first signs that a serious indigenous literary tradition was finally emerging in the independent Irish state. It was, of course, banned.

Born in 1935, McGahern grew up in Leitrim and Roscommon. His mother was a schoolteacher, his father a member of the Garda Síochána and most of his work evolves around the wildly disparate relationship he had with each of his parents.

His first two books, *The Barracks* published in 1963, and *The Dark*, 1965, are a fictionalised account of these relationships: the former with his mother, the latter with the father. They set the tone for McGahern's literary works – always featuring separately but merging at last in his final and possibly most accomplished work: *Memoir*, published just months before he died in 2006.

The impact of *The Dark* on the Ireland of 1965 can only be fully understood with reference to the social realities of the time. In a society where the authority of the Catholic Church and pater familias was absolute, the concepts of domestic violence and clerical abuse could not be exposed. In rural areas particularly, the victim of abuse, whether physical or sexual, had no support at all: the beaten child 'deserved it' and the raped woman 'was asking for it' and if they complained further they were ostracised or, worse, locked up.

The opening scene of *The Dark* is one of the most vivid

descriptions of domestic physical abuse in Irish literature. The narrator's father hears him using the word 'fuck' and takes him upstairs to punish him.

> 'Don't move and shut that shouting,' and when he was reasonably still except for the shivering and weeping, the leather came for the third time exactly as before. He didn't know anything or what he was doing or where the room was when the leather exploded on the black armrest where his ear was.

As the boy grows up, his hatred and mistrust of his father hardens. His only respite from near-constant fear is masturbation, but that only enhances his sense of guilt. Gradually, however, he senses that education could offer a way out and he eventually wins a scholarship which allows him freedom.

The catharsis of the novel, one of the more memorable scenes of the book, is when the boy, now a young adult, stands up to the father. It is so powerful that McGahern repeats the scene almost verbatim in *Memoir* – after forty years of writing not even he could improve on it.

McGahern was vilified by Church and state after the book's publication. He was, effectively, fired from his teaching job in Dublin and had to emigrate to London. Eventually he returned to Ireland and bought a farm near Aughawillan, County Leitrim, where his mother had taught. There he died from cancer in March 2006.

Lig Sinn i gCathú

BRENDÁN Ó HEITHIR

Ba Árannach, Gaillimheach, Éireannach agus Eorpach é Breandán
Ó hEithir agus bhí sé compordach le gach ceann de na lipéid sin.
Rugadh é ar Inis Mór, an t-oileán is mó de thrí oileán Árann, sa
bhliain 1930. Fuair sé a chuid oideachais i gcathair na Gaillimhe,
agus ina dhiaidh sin, bhí sé ina iriseoir do na nuachtáin náisiúnta
– an *Irish Press* agus an *Irish Times* ina measc – agus ina chraoltóir
teilifíse ar an gclár *Féach* a bhíodh ar Raidió Teilifís Éireann. Ba i
bPáras a chaith sé deireadh a shaoil.

Bhí an-cháil air mar iriseoir, go háirithe sna seachtainí roimh
na cluichí ceannais peile agus iománaíochta i bPáirc an Chrócaigh
agus aimsir an Olltoghacháin freisin.

Scríobh sé an-chuid leabhar i mBéarla agus i nGaeilge faoi
chúrsaí éagsúla agus bhí béim mhór aige ar an spórt agus ar an
bpolaitíocht. Ba é a chéad úrscéal *Lig Sin i gCathú* an leabhar
is tábhachtaí a scríobh sé. Nuair a foilsíodh é den chéad uair sa
bhliain 1976, ní raibh mórán díol ar leabhair Ghaeilge ach bhris
Lig Sin i gCathú an múnla sin. Ba é an chéad leabhar Gaeilge –
agus an t-aon leabhar ó shin i leith – a bhain áit amach ar liosta
na leabhar sárdhíola.

Cuirtear tús leis an úrscéal lenár laoch, Máirtín Ó Méalóid,
ag dul isteach geata Choláiste na hOllscoile i mBaile an Chaisil
(Gaillimh) chun a sheic scoláireachta a bhailiú. Nuair a deir an
doirseoir – a dtugtar an Púca air – leis gur chuala sé go raibh
Máirtín bailithe as an gcoláiste ar fad, aithníonn muid nach

mac léinn dícheallach atá sa Méalóideach. Ag an am céanna, mothaítear go bhfuil an-taithí ag gach éinne ar Mháirtín ach amháin Údaráis na hOllscoile.

Déardaoin dheireadh seachtaine na Cásca 1949 atá ann agus táthar chun Poblacht na hÉireann a fhógairt ar an Luan chun deireadh a chur le gunnadóireacht agus le foréigean. Is tábhachtaí do Mháirtín, áfach, an t-am atá le teacht ná an t-am atá caite. Feictear go bhfuil sé ag iarraidh a chuid neamhspleáchais féin a bhaint amach agus is anseo atá croí an úrscéil.

Leanann muid eachtraí Mháirtín i rith na deireadh seachtaine agus tugtar pictiúr bríomhar den saol a bhí i gcathair na Gaillimhe ag an am sin. Is leabhar greannmhar é seo freisin ina bhfuil an t-údar ag magadh faoin meánaicme agus faoin status quo.

Cloistear ceol na Gaeilge go soiléir in *Lig Sin i gCathú* agus feictear an deacracht a bhí ag an nglúin nua ag an am seo saoirse a bhaint amach.

One Voice: My Life in Song

Christy Moore

'How's it goin'?'

The deep rich voice behind me was full of warmth and generosity.

'Are ye still doing that gig for the blind?'

The car was at the back door, the guitar in the boot, could we go to the studio now? A quick phone call ahead and we were on our way.

Ten minutes later we were sitting in what we called the 'Echo Studio' in the university language lab and Seán gave us the nod. After strumming an introductory chord, Christy Moore launched with heart and vigour into 'The Cliffs of Doneen'.

The *Galway Echo* was a monthly talking newspaper for the blind edited by me, as a member of Galway Lions Club, and produced by Seán Mac Iomhair, Director of the Language Laboratory and Audio-Visual Services in NUIG. Every time Moore visited Galway he gave freely of his time and considerable talent to record a few songs for the *Echo*. It is a mark of the generosity of the man.

His book, *One Voice: My Life in Song*, is another.

In the preface, he tells us he never intended to write a book. However, during the early 1990s, having avoided several offers to have his story written, he got word that someone was writing an unauthorised version. This, as he says, put the wind up him, and his manager approached several publishers.

The problem was the starting point. Then, while the family was away on holidays, he began to put together all the songs he ever sang, along with comments on how he first heard them and when he first sang them. Suddenly he found he could revisit his life through the songs. This he did honestly and the book was completed.

First Moore gives us the full text of each song and then his own reaction. To complete the atmosphere, the book is illustrated with what seems like hundreds of black and white photographs relating to Moore's own personal life, his singing career, or some event relating to the specific song.

To enjoy the book fully the reader should resist flicking through it to find a favourite song and then putting it aside with the intention of reading it properly later. The real story of the book becomes apparent only when you begin at page one and work your way through it page by page. Gradually, a composite picture emerges s Moore lays his personal and artistic soul bare for us. It is an uplifting experience.

He writes:

> The best songs outlive the significance of their authors. It becomes incidental after a time, and the songs themselves reverberate down the years. Who wrote 'Lord Baker' or 'Raggle Taggle Gypsy' or who cares so long as the song helps us through the night.

In *One Voice*, Moore allows us a rare insight into the deep rich world of Irish song, its genesis, performance and impact on our daily lives. In giving his book an autobiographical slant, he ensures that not only the song but the singer lives on.

Stand and Give Challenge

Francis MacManus

There was a time, not so long ago, when Francis MacManus was a household name in Ireland. The only people who are aware of the name today are those who enter for the Francis MacManus Short Story Competition sponsored annually by RTÉ Radio.

Born in Kilkenny in 1909, MacManus was educated by the Christian Brothers before going to St Patrick's Drumcondra and University College Dublin. He taught school in Synge Street – one of his pupils was James Plunkett – for eighteen years before becoming Director of Talks and Features on Radio Éireann. All of this suggests a safe man in a safe time. MacManus appears to have had all the attributes of the respected Catholic nationalist who embodied the romanticised Ireland of de Valera's vision. In fact, while being religious, he never sought to impose his religious or political beliefs on his listeners or his readers.

In 1934, he published the novel *Stand and Give Challenge*, the first of a trilogy set in the Ireland of the penal days and based on the life of Clare poet, Donnacha Ruadh Mac Conmara, the subsequent novels being *Candle for the Proud* and *Men Withering*. The titles of his subsequent works have the same sense of Catholic triumphalism as was displayed on the banners that were in such prominent evidence during the Corpus Christi processions of the time.

When, however, his books are read closely a different image emerges, an image of the thinking independent man with a

steely sense of purpose and an ability to be objective in his own definition of patriotism and spirituality.

Stand and Give Challenge begins in an upstairs room of a Hamburg tavern some time in the early 1730s. Our hero is down to his last silver coin, desolate, bereft, homesick, when suddenly he hears below him a song being sung in a strange, unusual but immediately familiar language:

> There is honey on the trees in the misty vales
> Streams rilling in summer to the full of their ways,
> Waters gleaming there and dew at midday
> On the fair white hills of Éire.

The song inspires our hero to find himself a passage home and, despite his failure, being a 'spoiled priest', he makes his way painfully back to his native Clare and becomes the hedge schoolmaster in his own locality. There he seems set to finish out his days happily when famine strikes.

This sets off a whole new train of adventures which include all the elements of a good historical novel: romance, intrigue, elopement, press gangs, Jacobites and revolution. MacManus is a good storyteller and the narrative is clear and entertaining.

At the end of the story however, our hero and heroine do not go sailing off into the sunset. Throughout the book MacManus is constantly questioning the romantic version of the history of Ireland as taught by the emerging Irish state.

How Was it for You, Doctor?

Pat Ingoldsby

In his essay 'The Last Gleeman' first published in *The Celtic Twilight* in 1893, W.B. Yeats gives a potted biography of Michael Moran, better known in Dublin folklore as Zozimus. He describes him as being 'a true gleeman, being alike poet, jester and newsman of the people'.

Zozimus had a poem of his own called 'Moses' which 'went a little nearer poetry without going very near'. The first verse went:

> In Egypt's land, contagious to the Nile
> King Pharaoh's daughter went to bathe in style.
> She took her dip then walked unto the land
> To dry her royal pelt she ran along the sand.
> A bulrush tripped her, whereupon she saw
> A smiling babby in a wad of straw.

Despite Yeats's claim, Zozimus was not the last of the gleemen. Since his demise in 1843, the street poet, for that is essentially what Moran was, has remained a vital part of Irish cultural life, the raw edge of an underground literature – the chief celebrant of which today is Pat Ingoldsby.

True to the fierce independent tradition of the street poet, Ingoldsby is his own man. He is also a very private man. Once when asked about writing his autobiography he replied no, his

life had been lived: it was enough that he had done that and it should be left alone. Yet there is something in his demeanour that is candid and sympathetic.

Ingoldsby's work is not the stuff that academics will drool over, nor will it find its way into many poetry magazines, but this will not worry Ingoldsby.

His audience are the people who stop by wherever he has set up for the day and buy one or two books of his poetry. It is the driver of the bus full of people, which included Pat after a bad day's selling, who made the general announcement that the next stop would be the final stop as the bus was going for service and would everyone please disembark. 'Not you, Pat,' he finished, 'I'll take you home first.'

How Was it for You, Doctor? contains such gems as this:

> I was minding the rain
> Until I thought about
> Everything having a drink.
> The cracked earth
> The flowers
> The wet apples
> All drinking deep
> And saying
> 'God – that's lovely'
> And suddenly
> I didn't mind any more.

Go raibh a leithéid ann i gcónaí.

Some Experiences of an Irish R.M.

SOMERVILLE AND ROSS

Somehow, the image is irresistible. Two ladies sitting together in the parlour of the Big House, a long wet winter's evening stretching before them, bored, but with lively minds. They start to create together with mischievous glee the character of Major Yeates, Resident Magistrate, and the motley crew that was to people their wonderful stories, later published in book form under the title *Some Experiences of an Irish R.M.*

Of course, it didn't happen in this manner but the image is, nonetheless, irresistible. Edith Somerville and Violet Martin were second cousins in an old and well established Anglo-Irish family. They met for the first time in Castletownsend in 1886; Edith was then twenty-eight years of age and Violet, who was to adopt the literary pseudonym of Martin Ross, twenty-four. Together they formed what was to become one of the most intriguing and powerful partnerships of literature in English.

The first volume of *The Irish R.M.* was published in 1889 and was followed by two others, *Further Experiences of an Irish R.M.* (1908), and *In Mr Knox's Country* (1915). While these volumes may not be their most accomplished work (the laurels would generally go to *The Real Charlotte*) they were to become the hallmark of their literary reputation.

When we first meet Major Yeates, he is expounding to the lady who has just consented to be his wife the wonderful possibilities a resident magistracy in Ireland would offer them

Some Experiences of An Irish R.M.

BY
E. OE. Somerville,
AND
Martin Ross.

both – assuming, of course, that Philippa's (for that is the lady's name) godfather, who had been once a member of parliament, could swing the job for him.

The godfather delivers and next we find our hero resident for too long in the Skebawn's only hotel:

> My most immediate concern, as one who has spent nine weeks at Mrs Raverty's hotel will readily believe, was to leave it at the earliest opportunity; but in those nine weeks I had learned, amongst other painful things, a little, a very little, of the methods of the artisans in the West of Ireland. Finding a home had been easy enough. I had my choice of several, each with some hundreds of acres of shooting, thoroughly poached, and a considerable portion of the roof intact. I had selected one; the one that had the largest extent of roof in proportion to the shooting, and had been assured by my landlord that in a fortnight or so it would be fit for occupation.

The landlord turns out to be one Florry Knox who becomes Major Yeates's conduit with the rest of Ireland, and the spiritual, physical and moral life of the rest of Ireland seems to revolve around the noble pursuit of the fox.

What follows are among the funniest, irreverent and most delightful stories imaginable, full of spirit, mischief and laughter, with a little romance thrown in.

Home From England

JAMES RYAN

Perhaps the greatest symbol of the lethargy, hopelessness and uncertainty that prevailed in Ireland from the 1920s until the mid-1960s was the institution seen daily in the middle of every town and known colloquially as the 'corner boys'. The 'corner boys' were made up of anything from six to eight men who took up station at a strategic corner and never seemed to move for the whole day. Speech was limited to one sentence at a time, preferably at half-hourly intervals. None was ever seen to arrive or leave, yet there was changes of personnel throughout the day.

The 'corner boys' were to be avoided. Under no circumstances were you, as a child, to speak to them. In fact, if you had to pass them you were to cross to the other side of the street. And, if you were on your way to post a letter, you were under strict instructions to hold the envelope with the address pressed firmly to your chest. The less the 'corner boys' knew about your business the better.

In his first novel, *Home From England*, James Ryan gives the 'corner boys' a collective noun: 'The Moratorium.' It is a silent symbol ('The Moratorium' never speaks) that pervades the novel and every nuance of its movement is an indication of a shift of atmosphere within the village.

'The Moratorium' consists of men who had played (or claim to have played) an active part in the War of Independence and who now feel they have done their bit. They believe Ireland owes them

a living and are happy to watch the social fabric of the country disintegrate.

The action of the book opens with children at play during the late 1950s or early 1960s in an old ruin outside a rural village in Ireland. The subtle social differences between the boys are neatly delineated as the story unfolds.

The narrator's father is just home on his annual fortnight's holiday from England. There is an imperceptible change of mood in the house. His mother's social demeanour has upped a degree, there are whispers around town, and finally the news breaks formally – long after it was universally known – that the family is moving to England.

The journey across is superbly described. Every mile, every stop brings a change of mood that is noted as our travellers get closer to London. The realities of being Irish in London and the strangeness of it all brings the loneliness and alienation suffered by the adults into sharp focus.

Suddenly, the father receives a letter saying that his home-town is to honour him for his contribution to the War of Independence during the commemoration of the 50th Anniversary of the 1916 Rising. Now the whole family is travelling back home and the novel takes on a new energy.

Home From England is a book with many levels and needs to be read more than once. In discerning for the first time three separate social classes 'The Irish at Home,' 'The Irish in England' and the 'Home From England,' the author touches the truth: once an emigrant, always an emigrant.

Irish Tales of Mystery and Magic

Eddie Lenihan

The story has been told before but, like all good stories, deserves to be told again. Some years ago a boy in his late teens entered our shop, looking to buy a book as a birthday gift for his father. After I had made several unsuccessful suggestions, the options and the boy's patience were running out. I asked him who his father was.

'Eddie Lenihan,' he replied.

The gift was selected in an instant as I knew about Eddie's interest in the American Civil War so the book of the wonderful TV series, which had just then been screened, was the perfect choice. While the sale was being processed, I said: 'You must have had an amazing childhood.'

'Well, I'll tell you one thing, Mr Kenny, there was never anything in our house such as myth, 'twas always going to happen.'

For two generations of children (and adults), Eddie Lenihan has been something of an icon. He is small in stature, with bushy hair and a gruff exterior, and you only have to ask him if he has a story about Fionn Mac Cumhail, Biddy Early, or the 'Good People' (the 'Other Crowd,' as he calls them) to watch his eyes soften and his bearing lighten as he launches without hesitation into yet another magical and wonderful tale in the full and absolute conviction that these fantastic events did indeed take place.

Eddie's stories are not confined to our mythological or folk heroes and heroines. His intensity is such that he has the ability

to make the world of the 'other crowd' pertinent to the world of Ireland today. He once managed to have the building of a motorway diverted because pursuing its original path would have meant cutting down a fairy tree.

Thankfully, Mercier Press has remained faithful to Eddie by making his stories available in book form. Their latest offering, *Irish Tales of Mystery and Magic*, surpasses all previous publications.

We read of the adventures of 'Fionn Mac Cumhail in China', 'King Cormac's Fighting Academy', 'How the First Blackbird Came to Ireland', 'The Strange Case of Seán na Súl', 'Taoscán Mac Liath and the Magic Bees' and 'How Fionn Mac Cumhail made the Burren'. The book is sumptuously illustrated by Alan Clarke.

In his introduction, Eddie talks about the reality of the world of wonder, a world more readily appreciated by children than by adults. We were, he says, in danger of losing our sense of wonder, but the old stories are now making a comeback. He asks:

> How much better for a child to hear the tales of the Fianna than to sit day after day in front of the television? How much more exciting to hear of the exploits of Fionn Mac Cumhail or Toscán Mac Liath than be numbed by endless computer games?

The only real answer to these questions is to pick up the book and read it.

Watching the River Flow

EDITED BY THEO DORGAN AND NOEL DUFFY

Ireland has had its share of poets. A significant number have earned international recognition and three have won the Nobel Prize. The twentieth century has strong claims to be the golden era of Irish poetry but because there is such a wide variety of poets and, because of the elusive nature of poetry itself, it is difficult to find one anthology that will properly represent the breadth of verse, incorporating the disparate poetic traditions.

Aware of the difficulties involved, editors Theo Dorgan and Noel Duffy adopted a most unusual technique: they invited ten distinguished Irish poets to participate, allocating each one a specific decade and asking each to select the ten poems that were most characteristic of that particular decade, while supplying a preface with an explanatory introduction. The resulting anthology was published in 1999 by Poetry Ireland/Éigse Éireann with the title *Watching The River Flow – A Century of Irish Poetry*.

The first selection is made by Eavan Boland entitled '1900-1909: Beginnings,' followed by Eiléan Ní Chuilleanáin's '1910-1919: Changes and Translations,' Bernard O'Donoghue's '1920-1929: 'Who Speaks for These,' Thomas Kinsella's '1930-1939: The Nineteen Thirties,' Ciarán Carson's '1940-1949: Beagles, Horses, Bikes, Thighs, Boats, Grass, Bluebells, Rickshaws, Stockings,' John Montague's '1950-1959: Scylla & Charybdis,' Michael Longley's '1960-1969: A Boat On The River,' Seamus Heaney's '1970-1979: Meaning Business,' Cathal Ó Searcaigh's '1980-1989: In A State

100 poems selected by
Eavan Boland
Eiléan Ní Chuilleanáin
Bernard O'Donoghue
Thomas Kinsella
Ciaran Carson
John Montague
Michael Longley
Seamus Heaney
Cathal Ó Searcaigh
Nuala Ní Dhomhnaill
Edited by
Noel Duffy & Theo Dorgan

watchingthe*river**flow*

A Century in Irish Poetry

Of Flux' and Nuala Ní Dhomhnaill's '1990-1999: Tidal Surge'.

One of the book's more attractive elements is that, no matter how often it is read, it still contains treasures that surprise and delight. At this sitting, two such treasures were discovered. The first is from Louis MacNeice's 'Epilogues for W.H. Auden':

> Holidays should be like this,
> Free from over-emphasis,
> Time for soul to stretch and spit
> Before the world comes back on it.

The second is the first and last verse from Anthony Cronin's 'For a Father':

> With the exact length and pace of his father's stride
> The son walks,
> Echoes and intonations of his father's speech
> Are heard when he talks
>
> ...
>
> And now having chosen, with strangers,
> Half glad of his choice
> He smiles with his father's hesitant smile
> And speaks with his voice.

Talking to Ourselves

Ivor Kenny

This book has the following dedication:

> When he wanted to write a heavy editorial, my father
> would bring home his portable typewriter and close
> the door. Silence was enjoined. I breached the sanctum
> and got my nose above the edge of the dining room
> table. I asked, 'What are you doing?' 'I am writing an
> editorial.' 'Is it important?' 'It is. To me.'

The dedication is to the memory of the author's father T.J.W.
Kenny – founder, editor and managing director of the *Connacht
Tribune,* my grandfather. It was written by our uncle, Ivor
Kenny, edited by yours truly, bound by my brother Gerry and
published by Kenny's Bookshop and Art Gallery. It was, and is,
a family affair.

Subtitled 'Conversations with Editors of the Irish Media,' it is
the third volume of such conversations compiled by Ivor Kenny
and the only one published outside Dublin, in 1994. It consists
of interviews with the leading editors, in the Ireland of the time,
of all the major daily newspapers, north and south, of Sunday
newspapers, of a number of provincial newspapers (including the
Connacht Tribune) and the heads of news and current affairs in
RTÉ and BBC Northern Ireland, none of whom were women.
The book follows the same pattern as the other volumes in the

series – a photograph of the interviewee captioned with a succinct quotation, a biographical note and the interview.

The early career of each of the interviewees is neatly charted before the conversations move into the field of the profession's ethos. In every case, there is a strong sense of duty aligned with great pride in the work and a recognition of its important role in Irish society.

The whole tenor of the book is caught in the captions that accompany the photos of the interviewees. Vinnie Doyle (the *Irish Independent*) tells us, 'When it's going right, it's like drinking champagne all day – the most satisfying job in the world,' while Michael Brophy (the *Star*) simply states, 'all news is comment.' Michael Keane (the *Sunday Press*) believes that 'newspapers have a responsibility to be positive, not just to knock,' while Keith Baker (BBC Northern Ireland) is more forthright '...news is news, not image building. I don't see BBC News and Current Affairs in Northern Ireland as some ex-officio brand of the Northern Ireland Tourist Board.'

With the provincial press the focus changes. Kieran Walsh of the *Munster Express* boasts, 'You are not really dead until your name is in the death column of the *Munster Express*, while John Cunningham of the *Connacht Tribune* is equally bullish: 'Readers of provincial papers have a tremendous loyalty. I know families who would buy five *Connacht Tribune*s – four of them to be posted on a Thursday evening to sons and daughters living in England or America.'

The Last Invasion of Ireland

RICHARD HAYES

History is an exacting science requiring academic discipline. One of its great difficulties is that academic research can translate badly into general book form.

Fortunately for the public appetite, there comes a writer who, with all the proper credentials and necessary skills, can zoom in on one episode of history and produce a volume which informs, entertains and goes a long way towards revealing what happened, or at the very least captures the atmosphere and tensions that were in play. Such a writer is Richard Hayes. His book is *The Last Invasion of Ireland*, first published in 1937.

When General Humbert landed in Killala in north County Mayo on 22 August 1798 with 1,000 troops to assist the United Irishmen in their revolt against English rule, he was too late and in the wrong place. The rebellion was all but ended and the final pockets of resistance were on the other side of the country. After a brief campaign of six or seven weeks, Humbert surrendered to the English, was allowed to retain his military dignity, as were all his compatriots, and returned to France.

Born in Bruree, County Limerick, in 1882, Richard Hayes graduated from the Catholic University Medical School and became a dispensary doctor in Lusk, County Dublin. He was the commander of the Fingal Battalion of the Irish Volunteers and was arrested during Easter Week 1916, court-martialled and sentenced to death. His sentence was commuted to twenty

years' penal servitude and he was released in June 1917 under the general amnesty. He was rearrested in 1918 and, while in Reading Gaol, was elected MP for Limerick. Resigning from the Dáil in 1924, he devoted himself to his medical practice and to historical scholarship. He died in Dún Laoghaire in June 1958.

For professional historians, the General Humbert episode was little more than a postscript to the 1798 Rebellion. In this book, Richard Hayes brings those six weeks to life.

From the beginning, there is an immediacy in the narration. Hayes conveys the massive sense of excitement caused locally by the landing:

> On the morrow of the landing, Killala was full of tumult and animation. Good-humoured and high-spirited, the French soldiers in their bright uniforms thronged the little town jostling with frieze-coated natives, while the confused sounds of three languages blended and echoed along its narrowed streets.

Thousands of men from the countryside flocked to the colours:

> ...recruits continued to arrive with every hour – tall, broad-shouldered, fresh-faced men, contrasting in their physique with the lithe, sallow-faced soldiers of France...To those who were unprovided with pikes, the French distributed muskets and ammunition, while swords and pistols were handed out to their officers.

Hayes then goes on to describe how this raggle-taggle army went on to challenge the greatly superior British military presence in Ireland and the inevitable massacre that ensued.

The Road to Silence

Seán Dunne

There was an aura of reverence about Seán Dunne. Women were the first to sense it. Whenever he entered a room, conversation became respectfully muted. He had a deep warm smile and a calmness that bespoke fulfilment and was a balm to the senses. There was nothing but the warmest respect for Seán Dunne, the man, his work and his beliefs.

Dunne was born in Waterford in 1956. His mother died while he was still in national school and he was raised by his father, a childhood memorably recorded in the book *In My Father's House*. Educated by the Christian Brothers in Sion Hill Waterford, he then went to UCC before working as a reviewer and a journalist. He published several volumes of poetry and became literary editor of the *Cork Examiner*, in which capacity he gave many aspiring writers their first break.

It was, however, the mark of the man that the greatest legacy left to Irish literature appeared quietly and without fuss just two years before he died at the age of forty. *The Road to Silence*, subtitled 'An Irish Spiritual Odyssey', was published by New Island Books in 1994.

Despite the slightness of the volume, there is in its pages a moment or an image for each individual reader to savour and which will echo within their spiritual being. Its premise is neatly given in the first two paragraphs:

As a child, I saw the world with a religious dimension that I have never lost. At its most negative, this consisted of a morbid fear that punishment would ensue if I broke the rules of Catholicism…I desired to do good but not because I saw this as worthwhile in itself. Rather I feared that I might come to harm if I did otherwise. The threat of Hell lay behind every sinful action and affected me with such force that it can still haunt my mind. Even now, I am still not sure that the motives behind some of my actions and attitudes are free of this morbid fear, albeit in another form.

Like so many who grew up in the 1960s and 1970s, Dunne turns against the religion of his youth, but if he does he is never comfortable with the rejection, hence the journey which is the essence of the book. With warmth and candour, Dunne invites us to join him on the journey and we find ourselves doing it willingly and with open heart. It is a journey worth taking even if it is left simply at that. Perhaps the overall experience of the journey is best epitomised by Dunne himself in the final paragraph:

I learned a lot from each of these individuals and groups. My understanding of them was in direct descent from my visit to Mount Melleray in 1964 and it is a continuing discovery, a pilgrimage along a path that like Basho's Road to the far north of Japan, leads to a greater unity between what I am and what I do. Taken together, these places and lives form a kind of melody. When I am properly in tune with it, I know, with Julian of Norwich, that all manner of thing will be well.

Spanish Gold

G.A. Birmingham

One of the great enjoyments of a bookseller, more especially a second hand or antiquarian one, is that you never know what is going to happen next. There is never a dull moment. One such non-dull moment was when we opened a letter with a French stamp containing a handwritten letter ordering four first-edition George A. Birmingham novels from our catalogue. The letter was signed Graham Greene. How did Graham Greene ever hear of this – at least to English eyes – obscure writer from the west of Ireland?

The mystery deepens when we discovered that George A. Birmingham was a pseudonym for a Protestant rector, J. O. Hannay, who was born in Belfast and ministered in Westport from 1892 until 1913. Graham Greene's quest for Birmingham first editions continued – the orders always in the same clipped handwriting – until we completed the set.

Years later we heard that when Graham Greene was posted as a civil servant in Dublin, he, Paul Henry and George A. Birmingham holidayed in Achill and often went on the tear together. This piece of Achill folklore may or may not be true, but it certainly explains a great deal.

J.O. Hannay, born in Belfast in 1865, had an extraordinary career. After his stint in Westport he served as British chaplain to the British forces during the First World War, serving in France during 1916 and 1917. He was the author of nearly sixty comic

Spanish Gold
(1908)

George A. Birmingham

novels under his pseudonym as well as several religious books under his own name, some travelogues and one or two memoirs. In fact, nobody is sure how much he actually wrote. He turned to writing novels in 1905 to support a meagre income and it was the publication of *Spanish Gold* in 1908 that established his popularity.

The Reverend Joseph John Meldon, curate of Ballmoy, is riding furiously along the road out of the town when there is no reason at all to hurry. But then the Rev. J.J. Meldon is a man of impetuous energy, confident of his own genius and not at all what one would expect of a country curate. There follows a motley crew of characters such as Major Kent, Thomas O'Flaherty Pat, Mary Kate his granddaughter, Higginbotham, the English civil servant, Euseby Langton and Sir Giles (the perceived villains of the piece), the smell of 'Spanish Gold', and a dubious diary. Throw in a chief secretary, add one or two other ingredients, and the scene is set.

In the midst of all this mayhem, surprisingly, there are some serious social issues raised such as the following extraordinary outburst from Meldon:

> We're on the brink of a revolution – the biggest thing that there has ever been. And the cause of it is the concentration of wealth in the hands of a few people who are using it for purely selfish purposes...Now what is our duty under the circumstances? What is the duty of every well-disposed person who values the stability of civilisation? Obviously it is to prevent the selfish, depraved and fundamentally immoral people from acquiring wealth; to see that only the well-intentioned and public-spirited get rich.

Strumpet City

James Plunkett

At 3.15 am, with special quiet, His Majesty's yacht *Victoria and Albert* approached the harbour mouth and lay to. And at half past six, with the first light, the workmen had finished. They looked with some pride on the result of their labours. The floral arch was ready for the disembarkation. It stood mute and beautiful at the harbour mouth, its green leaves stirring a little in the dawn breeze, its crimson and gold banner announcing the warm welcome of the citizens with the words, 'Come back to Erin'; 'God Bless Our King.'

This seemingly simple paragraph begins what is one of the finest historical novels ever written in any language. Its almost idyllic atmosphere belies the power and strength of what is in store for the reader. Rarely in any language has a novel achieved and sustained the intensity of trauma and movement – conveyed in such a simple and direct language – as James Plunkett's *Strumpet City* does, and it is noteworthy too in that it went into a second printing before the first one was published.

Born in 1920 and reared in Dublin, James Plunkett Kelly was educated in Synge Street and the College of Music. At seventeen, he became a clerk in the Dublin Gaslight Company and was soon an active trade unionist, working for a time under Jim Larkin.

In 1955 he joined Radio Éireann and subsequently became a television producer for RTÉ. He is the author of a collection of short stories, a volume of essays, a travelogue, some plays and two novels. *Strumpet City*, published in 1969, is by far his finest work. It is set in Dublin, beginning with the royal visit in 1907 and ending with the onset of the First World War in 1914. Ostensibly the love story of Mary and Fitz, their courtship, wedding and their married life together in a Dublin tenement until Fitz enlists in the British Army, the novel revolves around the Dublin Lockout in 1913 and its effects on the social fabric of the capital city.

An extraordinary feature of the novel is the facility with which the narration moves from social class to social class. Plunkett introduces a wide variety of fascinating and colourful characters. While the main theme of the book is the struggle between the capitalists of Dublin represented by the overpowering figure of William Martin Murphy and the fledgling trade union movement whose champion is the ever-resourceful James Larkin, its main focus is on the thousands of lives that are affected by this struggle, the demands it makes on their courage and humanity and the way it exposes hypocrisy and inhumanity.

Symptomatic of this struggle between rich and poor is the antagonism between Father O'Connor, the sanctimonious, snobbish young priest – who has been moved from the wealthy parish of Kingstown to the desperately poor parish of St Brigid's in the city – and the street-wise Father Giffley. The conservative Catholicism of the former is soon at odds with the more humane and forgiving pastoral administration of the latter, particularly in relation to the treatment of Rashers Tierney, one of the most memorable characters in modern Irish literature. It is the tragic fate suffered by Rashers as a result of this struggle that underlines the tragedy suffered by Dublin as it tries to drag itself into the twentieth century.

Castle Rackrent

MARIA EDGEWORTH

The most striking aspect of *Castle Rackrent*, first published in 1800, is not the fact that the author is female writing at a time when a woman's role was most definitely confined to domestic chores and the bearing of children, when any excursion by a female into the intellectual or literary arena could only be, it was thought, of a frivolous and inconsequential nature. What strikes the reader is the directness of the attack by the author in her introduction on the literary pretentiousness of academic historians and their manifest inability to describe what really happened and why:

> The prevailing taste of the public for anecdote has been censured and ridiculed by critics, who aspire to the character of superior wisdom: but if we consider it in a proper point of view, this taste is an incontestable proof of the good sense and profoundly philosophic temper of the present times. Of the number who study, or at least who read history, how few derive any advantage from their labours! The heroes of history are so decked out by the fine fancy of the professed historian; they talk in such measured prose, and act from such sublime or such diabolical motives, that few have sufficient taste or heroism, to sympathise in their fate.

Edgeworth continues to berate so-called historians for not allowing the reader see behind the scenes, and makes the case that in the context of their flowery style and inability to discriminate character, the simple tale told by our illiterate narrator in the vernacular could be nothing else but the authentic truth. So we are introduced to Honest Thady Quirk.

In the characteristic style of the *seanchaí*, Thady presents himself as a poor but honest man, and then stresses the ancient nobility of his lifelong patrons, the Rackrents: 'Everybody knows this is not the old family name, which was O'Shaughlin, related to the Kings of Ireland – but that was before my time.'

The scene is thus set for what is considered to be the first historical novel in the English language. Our narrator brings us through four heads of the Rackrent Estate, each more feckless and dissolute then the last, until finally the estate is in ruins. The Rackrents are seen as the victims rather than the architects of their own downfall and the real villain of the piece is none other than the son of our narrator: 'he is a high gentleman, and never minds what poor Thady says, and having better than £1500 a year, landed estate, looks down upon honest Thady, but I wash my hands of his doings...'

The ironic tone is sustained right through the novel, which has many parallels with Voltaire's *Candide*. One senses that the author is enjoying herself immensely and it is this sense of humour, along with the extraordinary writing skills manifest in the narration that gives the book its extra lift.

The Stories

Frank O'Connor

One late afternoon during the late 1940s, or early 1950s, a tall imposing man with a massive head of white hair came into the shop and, as she said herself, 'without as much as a by your leave or anything like that,' asked Mother who were the three best Irish short-story writers of the day. 'Liam O'Flaherty, Sean O'Faolain and Frank O'Connor,' she answered truthfully. The man left abruptly. 'I don't think he even said a thank you, a good evening or a good night.'

Some weeks later, while reading the *Irish Times*, she came upon a photo of her interlocutor, 'spread,' as she says, 'right across the page', with a caption telling her that her rather rude visitor was none other than Frank O'Connor. She, in the best tradition, was mortified. She never did forgive him, but was always quick to add, her love of books and literature coming to the fore, that 'his stories made up a great deal for him'.

Michael O'Donovan, who wrote under the pseudonym of Frank O'Connor, was born in Cork in 1903. His childhood was spent largely with his mother. His father, a British soldier, was mostly absent. His formal schooling stopped at twelve years of age but continued informally under the tutelage of Daniel Corkery, who directed him towards the Russian writers, Gaelic poetry and nationalism. He took the Republican side during the Civil War and was interned in Gormanstown. After that he became a librarian, a director of the Abbey Theatre, a travelling academic

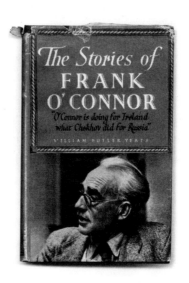

The Stories of
FRANK
O'CONNOR

"O'Connor is doing for Ireland
what Chekhov did for Russia"

WILLIAM BUTLER YEATS

but, most of all, one of the most celebrated short-story writers in any language.

There is in O'Connor a sense of self-deprecation which surfaces in his introduction to this volume, but we are not always sure whether the author is laughing at the reader or at himself. He tells us that being asked to gather all his best stories in one book is something he has always secretly longed for. Then, in the next sentence, he says that for this reason, he has excluded everything from his first book *Guests of the Nation*.

Happily, the collection is nonetheless an excellent collection of first-rate stories written by O'Connor, stories which have established him as, possibly, the finest short-story writer ever. The book opens with the stunning first paragraph of 'My Oedipus Complex':

> Father was in the army all through the war – the first war – so, up to the age of five, I never saw much of him, and what I saw did not worry me.

This collection, first published in 1953 by Hamish Hamilton, has such wonderful classics as 'First Confession', 'Nuns for the Church', 'Don Juan's Temptation', 'The Majesty of the Law' and 'The Idealist'.

All the stories are imbued with O'Connor's wonderful sense of humanity, a high degree of humour and a style of English that sings with a lilting Cork accent.

The Island of Ghosts

EILÍS DILLON

June of 1962 was one of the wettest on record. Out of sheer boredom, I picked up a book by Fergal McGrath SJ called *Adventure Island* and, because the opening scene spoke of a twelve-year-old in Galway who was bored during a wet summer, I began to read. I was soon engrossed by its story line.

Many years later, in 1989, a children's novel called *The Island of Ghosts* was published and, although much older, I read it from cover to cover with tremendous pleasure for two reasons: I had greatly enjoyed a historical novel by the same author entitled *Across the Bitter Sea* published sixteen years earlier and the story line was every bit as engrossing as that of *Adventure Island*.

Eilís Dillon was born in Galway in 1920, and while she had a respectable reputation as a novelist and academic, as well as being the author of some lesser-known detective books, her more solid claim to fame is as a writer of children's books, most notable of which are *The Island of Horses*, *The Singing Cave* and the award-winning *The Island of Ghosts*.

> Until the time had almost come to leave our island, I had never thought much about what this would mean. Sometimes I would feel a shiver of excitement run through me, as if some strange thing was about to happen, and then I might pause for a second to wonder what my new life would be. But I was usually too busy

to bother with it. Other people left to go to boarding school, as I was meant to do, or to their uncles and aunts and cousins in Portland, Maine, or to find work in Dublin, if they were not needed at home. It was the natural thing.

This opening paragraph contains the words of Dara Faherty, the son of the post master on Inishglass Island at the mouth of Galway Bay. Since childhood Dara and his sister Barbara have been best friends with Brendan Connolly and his sister Cáit

As our tale begins, the boys are finishing their formal schooling on the island and their teacher Mr Lennon is preparing them for the scholarship exams that will allow them to continue their education in Galway. However, Mr Lennon is not reputed to be the best of teachers. In steps the mysterious Mr Webb – whose local nickname is 'Bardal', the Irish for drake – who gives the boys private tuition that enables them to win the scholarships. The story takes an unexpected twist and as it develops the book acquires a deeper dimension and the boys find themselves questioning their own destiny and future.

Dillon also brings into play the traditions and suspicions of an island culture and the difficulties this culture faces as the outside world impinges on it more and more. *The Island of Ghosts* is not just a classic children's novel, it questions the extent to which an island culture can be modernised before it is irretrievably damaged.

Knocknagow

CHARLES J. KICKHAM

First published in 1879, *Knocknagow or The Homes of Tipperary* was to become the popular Bible of respectable nationalism and, along with the picture of the Sacred Heart, the photo of Pádraic Pearse and of the current Pope, it had a place around the fireside of every Catholic homestead in the Irish Free State. It was certainly the most requested book in our shop during the 1970s and 1980s. Since then, its popularity has faded but it retains its iconic status right into the twenty-first century.

Kickham was born at Cnocneeagaw near Mullinahone, County Tipperary, in 1828, the son of a prosperous shopkeeper. His was a strongly nationalist family (his uncle was John O'Mahony, a co-founder of the Fenians in the US) and he was strongly influenced by the political rhetoric of the Young Ireland movement. He became an active figure in Charles Gavan Duffy's Tenant League of the 1850s.

In 1860 he became a sworn member of the Fenian Brotherhood and was arrested along with all its leaders in 1865. He was sentenced to fourteen years in prison but was released in the general amnesty of 1869 and thereafter, until his death in 1882, he pursued a literary career.

As a work of literature, *Knocknagow* wouldn't win any prizes. It is overwritten, it borders on the sentimental, and, on a number of occasions, the author seems to lose control of his plot.

Despite all this, the story holds and what emerges is a genuine

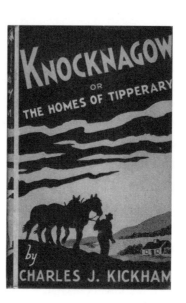

and strong tale set in the Ireland of the 1870s, when famine was still an annual threat, and all parties living on the land were vulnerable to eviction and ruin no matter how prosperous and hardworking they appeared to be. We see how a strong traditional culture is undermined and then finally destroyed by avaricious and cruel landlords and their unscrupulous agents.

Mr Henry Lowe, the landlord's nephew, stays as the guest with the Kearneys, one of the more successful tenant families. They introduce him to the homes of Tipperary and he comes to know and respect the religious, cultural and social ethos of the people.

As the narration proceeds Lowe himself is thrust into the background and we meet such memorable characters as Barney 'Wattletoes' Broderick, Mat the Thrasher, and the Tailor Lahy with his constant craving for 'a little nourishment'. The novel ends with the disintegration of this society and the ruin of the relatively prosperous Kearneys, victims of the corrupt land system.

With all of its Victorian anachronisms, 'Knocknagow' is probably mostly read today in an abridged edition. For all of that, it remains one of the best descriptions in Irish literature of rural Ireland just prior to the Land War.

The Hungry Grass

RICHARD POWER

He dreamt that night he was in a wood, rooted at the spot. A wind blew, branches thrashed, the trees strained all around him. Leaves began to fall, slowly at first, then, gathering force, until a tempest of leaves rushed past him. They filled the spaces between the trees, moving with a strange sound like the distant drumming of hooves. The sound grew louder and louder until it seemed that the whole wood was on the move, galloping away from him. Then the sound died away into the distance and he was left standing alone.

In this remarkable passage, Tom Conroy, a parish priest working somewhere in the west of Ireland, and the main protagonist of Richard Power's novel *The Hungry Grass* (first published in 1969), comes to realise the full depth of his loneliness and isolation. The title of the book derives from an Irish superstition that whoever walks on the grass where a Famine victim fell will himself be tormented by hunger.

Richard Power is not well known. Born in Dublin in 1924, he was educated by the Christian Brothers before joining the civil service in 1945. He took leave of absence to go to TCD and learn Irish. He is the author of three books: *Úll i mBarr an Ghéagáin* (1959), later translated by Victor Power as *Apple in the Treetop, In*

RICHARD POWER

The
Hungry
Grass

the Land of Youth (1964) and *The Hungry Grass*. He died in 1970.

The Hungry Grass begins with Fr Tom Conroy's funeral. That he should choose their annual ordination-reunion dinner as the hour of his death was seen by his clerical colleagues as a final example of the man's genius for causing trouble, an inconvenience more especially disturbing to Fr Mahon, at whom his final enigmatic smile had been directed. Conroy has appointed Mahon to be his executor and when Mahon goes to Conroy's house he finds it in a state of disarray, with strong evidence that Conroy has had a drink problem. Most disturbing of all is Mahon's discovery of a hidden cupboard in which there are dozens and dozens of jars, all crammed with crumpled-up bank notes.

Mahon quickly fulfills his duties as executor and gradually forgets Conroy, except for once when he hears a reading from the life of St Theresa of Avila,

> It was the saint's description of how she dreamt of hell in the shape of a muddy path leading to a cupboard in a wall. For a moment, Conroy seemed somewhere there, just a brief indistinct glimpse of him with head lowered as if he were searching for something.

The body of the book is a description of that search during the last year of Conroy's life. Realising that his death is imminent, Conroy searches for a sense of fulfillment and belonging. Everything about him – his family, his clerical colleagues, his own parishioners, even his own faith – suggests that all he has touched, except for the odd pyrrhic victory, has been a failure and that his own work as a pastor has been meaningless. One last frantic trip to England, to become reconciled with the long-lost sons of his dead brother and to redress a family injustice done to them, ends in disaster and Conroy returns home to die.

The Moynihan Brothers in Peace and War

Edited by Deirdre McMahon

The Moynihans were a prominent Tralee family at the beginning of the twentieth century. Maurice, the father, was active in local trade and politics and, because of his political activities, came to the notice of the RIC on a number of occasions.

In 1890, he married Mary Power and they had six children. Michael, the eldest, was the apple of his mother's eye and presents an austere, almost overbearing mien. John, Michael's junior by a year, is a more open character, although he too is imbued with the conservative mores of the period.

Michael was one of the increasing number of Catholics from small-farm and trade backgrounds to benefit from the Intermediate Act of 1878 and received a post-primary education, as a result of which he went to University College Dublin in 1908. In 1910 he left UCD without a degree and joined the Home Civil Service. He was based at first in Dublin before being transferred to Croydon in the autumn of 1913. On 2 March 1914, Michael enlisted in the Civil Service Rifle, a territorial unit of the London Regiment. In 1916, he signed up for foreign service and, at the end of June was transferred to France just before the Battle of the Somme. He was killed on 3 June 1918, five months before the Armistice.

The book *The Moynihan Brothers in Peace and War 1908-1918* comprises correspondence mainly between Michael and John from the time Michael went to Dublin until his death in June

The
Moynihan Brothers
in Peace and War 1909–1918

THEIR NEW IRELAND

Edited and introduced by **DEIRDRE McMAHON**

1918. Subtitled 'Their New Ireland', the correspondence provides a vivid portrait of a large and close family during a tumultuous period in Irish history. Although the brothers always remain close, one senses the tensions between the austere Michael, whose politics are right-wing, anti-suffragette and conservative, and the more lenient John, who has strong nationalist tendencies, especially after the 1916 Rising.

There are also occasional letters to Michael from his mother – the heartbeat of the book – and other members of the family, and there is the odd interjection of a newspaper announcement relating to the family or an official letter from the authorities.

The book is completed with a long and informative introduction by the editor Deirdre McMahon, a short epilogue and a series of most helpful notes.

In all, the reader is presented with a wonderful portrait of daily life as lived by an ordinary family in Ireland at the beginning of the twentieth century.

One can sense Mary Moynihan's helplessness and fears when she writes to her son in July 1914:

> I hope you will not get cold camping out. Be sure &
> send home socks to be washed. I shall send them back
> by return of post. The weather is still awful...

The Moynihan Brothers in Peace and War is a powerful record of the effect momentous international events have on the daily lives of people.

Light a Penny Candle

MAEVE BINCHY

For the bookseller, having Maeve Binchy to sign books is something of a mixed blessing. On the positive side, there will be a massive turnout, a queue to the door, and a buzz that can only be good for business. The catch is that the queue is slow-moving and there is a time limit to the book signing. You see, Maeve's generosity of spirit, her openness of heart, her genuine interest in everybody are such that few people can meet her without telling her their life story, even at a public book signing. Furthermore there is a tendency to divulge one's innermost secrets but no matter how evil or devious one has been, Maeve's warm welcome is all-forgiving and all troubles seem to disappear. Nobody leaves Maeve Binchy's company without a smile.

The bookseller needn't worry too much, though. Maeve, the adept professional, keeps the queue moving, lots of books are sold and everyone is happy.

Born in Dublin in 1940 and educated in the Holy Child Convent in Killiney and at UCD, Maeve Binchy taught for a while before joining *The Irish Times*. The warmth of her writing was soon noticed, especially her ability to humanise august events such as a royal wedding, and there were a number of reprints of her articles in book form. It could be said, however, that *Light a Penny Candle* was her first real book. Certainly when it was published in 1982, it was the first serious Irish bestseller, and it opened a whole new world for Irish women writing for a popular audience.

Light a Penny Candle tells the story of two girls, Aisling and Elizabeth. Elizabeth, the only child in a loveless marriage, lives in London. The Second World War has just started and there is the need to evacuate all children to the country. Elizabeth's parents have no relatives they can turn to and so are in a quandary. Then her mother remembers a school friend called Eileen who lives in Ireland and who now has a sizeable family. A letter is written, an invitation extended and timid Elizabeth goes to live with the boisterous O'Connors in Ireland, the most boisterous member being a girl her own age called Aisling.

The two girls become blood sisters, best friends and inseparable companions. After the war Elizabeth returns to England – where her parents are on the point of breaking up – but the girls' friendship survives the separation and the book follows their lives, joys, loves and tribulations over the next twenty years.

Binchy is an inveterate storyteller with a magic gift for dialogue. Her ear is so sensitive that she catches the nuances between the English as spoken in the reserved almost severe accents of Elizabeth's English home in London and the more energetic language of the Irish O'Connors. This allows her the space to gently satirise the mores of both nations and this she does with great glee.

Perhaps the greatest charm of the book, however, is the intimate tone achieved by the author. The reader feels that Binchy's story is for their ears only. This adds to the book a delicious sense of conspiracy, an almost childish delight in a secret shared.

The Ancient Books of Ireland

Michael Slavin

There are books that are written to tell a story, to reveal a truth about the human condition, to preach a new religion or philosophy, or to uncover a historic event. And then there are books, like *The Ancient Books of Ireland*, that are a labour of love.

By all accounts a Meath man, Michael Slavin has already published a number of books on Tara, and one on Irish show jumpers. He is a recognised expert on Irish equestrianism.

In this book, Slavin deals separately with sixteen of our ancient books – beginning with the *Cathach*, Ireland's oldest surviving book (written at the beginning of the seventh century) and ending with Keating's *Foras Feasa ar Éirinn*, written in the 17th century. He describes the place and the writing of each book, the circumstances of its authorship, the story of its survival and its present condition.

Profusely illustrated throughout, the book is full of delectable asides and vignettes. Describing the contents of the *Yellow Book of Lecan* (1391) we are told: 'The expulsion of the Deisi tribe from Tara is recounted, along with further stories about Conor Mac Neasa, King of Ulster. An account of the inter-regal strife that ended in the destruction of the royal Leinster site of Dind Righ is here. And, reflecting some of the more widespread interest of the time, stories of Greek and Roman heroes are included as well.'

With regards to *The Book of Armagh* (*c.* 807), the belief that it was written by St Patrick was strengthened by the words on

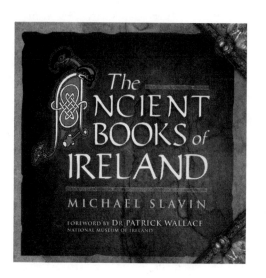

The
ANCIENT
BOOKS of
IRELAND

MICHAEL SLAVIN

FOREWORD BY DR PATRICK WALLACE
NATIONAL MUSEUM OF IRELAND

folio 24: 'Thus far the book which Patrick wrote with his own hand; and on the 17th day of March Patrick went to Heaven.' From this passage we inherited our national holiday, although the contention that Patrick was the book's author is now largely discounted. Of the many legends that surround the *Cathach* and its purported author, St Colmcille, the most famous is the dispute that resulted in the copyright ruling given by the King of Tara, Dermot Mac Cerball, grandson of Niall of the Nine Hostages, against the saint: 'To every cow its calf, to every book its copy.'

The Book of Lismore (1480) enumerates the ten conditions a warrior had to fulfill before being accepted into the Fianna:

1. He had to be a poet.
2. He had to fight off nine attacking warriors without being wounded, while restrained in a hole in the ground.
3. With just the distance of one tree as a head start, he must evade pursuers, while running through one of the chief woods of Ireland.
4. Not a hair from his woven head must be found on a tree in the wood.
5. While running, his weapon must not tremble in his hand.
6. He should not break even a withered stick under foot.
7. He must be able to stoop under a branch as low as his knee.
8. He must leap a branch as high as his ear.
9. He should be able to pluck out a thorn from his heel without breaking his stride.
10. His family should pledge not to sue his slayer in combat.

The Burning of Bridget Cleary

Angela Bourke

Towards the end of 1999, an imminent eclipse that was out of the ordinary attracted a great deal of coverage in the media: the best vantage points to view it from, the possible eye damage it could cause, the Celtic overtones (or undertones) – the paraphernalia of a human race preoccupied with its own importance.

What was striking about the eclipse itself was the silence that prevailed. Hushed by the ominous darkness that suddenly fell, the world seemed to take a deep breath and behold the real elements that govern our lives and over which we have absolutely no control – light and dark, of water, air, fire and stone. I remember at the time thinking, despite the great technological breakthroughs, the landing on the moon, the wonderful developments in medicine and the huge improvements in the quality of life throughout the western world, how little the human being has progressed, how fragile we really are when faced with the true force of nature and how we can still subscribe to only two absolute truths, those of birth and death.

It was a matter of some coincidence that Angela Bourke's book *The Burning of Bridget Cleary* should have been published at around the same time. In this book we are once again at the end of a century. Once again we witness a society congratulating itself on giant steps of progress and on its absolute certainty of its own self-righteousness. Once again, we see humanity being compelled to face the forces that shape it and we see this confrontation

ending in confusion and bewilderment.

The Burning of Bridget Cleary takes us back to County Tipperary in the 1890s. Bridget, wife of Michael Cleary, falls ill. The illness worsens and the husband travels long distances on foot (and in horrific weather) to seek the care of the doctor and the priest. His appeals are ignored by both. He then has recourse to a folk doctor living up the mountain who prescribes some herbal medicine. When this does not seem to work, the notion gradually emerges that the body in the bed is not Bridget Cleary at all but a changeling and that the real Bridget Cleary is away with the fairies.

As this idea takes hold of the minds of those nursing the sick woman, so does the idea of traditional folk cure, purification by fire. Eventually those present lift the body and pass it over the open fire with a view to exorcising the changeling. Having suffered this ordeal, the victim seems to be recovering (the herbal medicine apparently now taking effect). The following evening the husband, in a frenzy, repeats the purification by fire ordeal and causes the death of Bridget Cleary. The rest of the book is an account of the subsequent trial.

Angela Bourke gives us pen-portraits of all the protagonists along with superb insights into their actions and their motivations. We watch Michael Cleary attempting to have his wife cured by civilised means and, when he finds that door shut in his face, having recourse to the folk beliefs that are second nature to him. We see how civilised society deals with the situation, its bewilderment at the savagery of Cleary's actions and its attempts to explain them, using the criteria of a 'new' science: anthropology.

A Hidden Church

LIAM SWORDS

In the sanitised version of Irish history taught in Irish schools there were two events which became the main symbols of English atrocities towards Ireland, so much so that they often become confused with each other: the Cromwellian campaign and the Penal Laws. According to this version of our past, these two events demonstrate more than any others England's treachery and evil intent as against Ireland's strength of character and loyalty to the One True Faith. This perception was the foundation stone of the negative attitude of modern Ireland towards England.

While the Cromwellian campaign was well documented – particularly its most bloodthirsty episodes – there was little available, outside vague references to the more oppressive acts, in relation to the Penal Laws.

Curiously, the same situation still exists. Books relating to the eighteenth century tend to discuss the literary achievements of Swift and Goldsmith, the architectural splendour of Georgian Dublin and the political philosophy and oratory of Grattan and Burke. Outside a small pamphlet by Maureen Wall entitled *The Penal Laws*, published in the 1960s, there was nothing else until Columba Press published Liam Sword's *A Hidden Church* in 1997. Subtitled 'The Diocese of Achonry 1689-1818', the first volume of a history of that diocese, the book is an in-depth study of political, economic, social, religious and cultural life in Ireland while the Penal Laws held sway.

A priest of the diocese of Achonry, Liam Swords spent much of his ministry in Europe where he was the archivist of the Collège des Irlandais and chaplain to the Irish in Paris. He has published several volumes on the Irish diaspora in France as well as the three-volume history of Achonry.

In *A Hidden Church* Liam Swords systematically uncovers the Ireland of the Penal days. Chapter One, entitled *'Dlithe na nGall'*, deals with political events from 1689 to 1758 and mainly concerns the enactment and execution of the laws, while Chapter Two, *'Dóchas'*, describes their dismantling. Chapters Three and Four, *'Ó Rí go Rámhainn'* and *'Saol na nDaoine'* deal with life on the land and the everyday life of the people, and from there we move to *'Clann na nGall'*, the life of Protestants, and *'An Scoláire Bocht'*, the educational opportunities for Catholics.

As their education involved considerable expense and almost certainly a sojourn in Europe, as described in *'Des Messes et Des Arguments'*, priests were largely recruited from the wealthier families, then becoming the religious icons of Catholic nationalist Ireland known as the 'Soggarth Aroon'.

The rest of the book is taken up with the life of the ordinary people and their religious practices under the régime. *'B'fhéidir le Dia'* is a chapter on the bishops of the diocese from 1707 to 1808 with the English subtitle 'Occasional Visitors' and two chapters deal with the final throes of the Penal Laws.

A Hidden Church is a seismic book of Irish history about society in the eighteenth century. It suggests that, although oppressed and suffering, the Irish peasant was not perhaps as impoverished as his European counterpart and retained throughout a degree of political and cultural sophistication uncharacteristic of a downtrodden people.

The White Page/An Bhileog Bhán

EDITED BY JOAN McBREEN

In Ireland, the female contribution to literature did not surface until the beginning of the nineteenth century. With the publication of novels by Maria Edgeworth and Lady Morgan, the value of that contribution was established, although it received only sporadic recognition during the rest of that century. If female prose writers found it difficult to attract attention, it was even tougher for poets.

The same situation, though not as severe, pertained throughout the twentieth century. However, with the relaxing of censorship in the 1960s and the growth of the women's movement in the 1970s, the contribution of women to Irish poetry is at last being properly valued.

In her dual-language anthology, *The White Page/An Bhileog Bhán*, published by Salmon Press in 1999 and subtitled 'Twentieth Century Irish Women Poets', Joan McBreen documents the Irish female poetic voice of the twentieth century. The book is, in effect, a biographical dictionary of more than a hundred Irish women poets who have published at least one collection. Each entry consists of a biographical note, a photo of the poet if available and one poem.

Two poems in this collection epitomise the aspiration and more particularly (in the aesthetic and pragmatic sense) the task of the woman poet. The first, from Donegal-born Anna Marie Dowdican, is entitled 'Mine Be':

THE WHITE PAGE
An Bhileog Bhán
Twentieth-Century Irish Women Poets

Joan McBreen

Mine be the strength of courage deep
Rushing swelling alive and free.
Mine be the faithfulness of the turning tide
The hidden depths of the green salt sea.

Mine be the silence of lonely hills
To face softened mists of grey shadow.

Mine be the brimming furnace of fire's core
The love of all and all and more.

Mine be the life of veiled glances
The sighing winds and mystic trances.
…
Mine be the life to live beyond poetic thought…

The second, 'Ná Caoin', is by Aran-born Máire Uí Nuanáin:

Scríobh dán grinn adúirt tú
le muid a chur le gáire
ach ní féidir leis an ngáire a theacht
go mbíonn an brón ligthe.

Trí gáir ar cnoc
A lig clan Tuireann
Trí gáir ar cnoc
Leis an mbrón a ligean

Lig dom mar sin mo bhrón a ligean
Agus nuair a bheas mo chroí ar nós an linbh
Inseoid duit dán
A chuirfeas ionat dinglis.

Echoes of a Savage Land

Joe McGowan

No matter what way we look at it, clichés or no clichés, we are more ruled by nature than we realise and no amount of modernisation or scientific endeavour is going to change that. For all the comforts we now enjoy, nature has a habit of showing who the real boss is and no amount of forecasting or human prevention is going to gainsay it. Watch an angry sea crash against mountains of protective barriers and see how puny we are against such real power.

In the cities and towns we grow farther and farther away from these realities and depend more and more on those few (and fewer) people living on the land to remind us of their significance. Our landscape exudes a poetry we sometimes fail to understand so our dependence on a competent interpreter grows. Such an interpreter is Joe McGowan from Mullaghmore, County Sligo, whose book, *Echoes of a Savage Land*, published in 2001, details man's struggle with the land, the sea, the sky and the wildlife that feeds and nurtures him. Most of the customs described in the book are disappearing: within a generation they will be the stuff of folk history.

This is, however, no sentimental journey, bemoaning what is lost; it is a real telling of the tension between the old and the new, the author himself sometimes being drawn towards the new, even if reluctantly. In a way, this is the charm of the book. This frank struggle is constant and sometimes finds comic expression

as in the description of the author not wanting to twist the rope for his father when he could be in his neighbour's house instead, listening – on the only radio in the neighbourhood – to the latest Perry Mason adventure.

Echoes of a Savage Land takes on the rhythm of a fireside conversation and gathers together, without ostentation, the wisdom of the author's predecessors. For example we are told that the poet and the dreamer weren't the best workers. You cannot write poetry and pick potatoes at the same time. As with all good conversations, the authorities referred to are not exclusive to the twentieth century, or indeed to Ireland. The narrative is sprinkled with Shakespearean and Chaucerian quotations. We are treated to descriptions of Islamic and Jewish as well as Nordic and Celtic traditions.

The book is replete with stories of this world and the next. We meet the devil on several occasions, we see deceased loved ones reappear, we hear of other people being spirited away. Remedies for toothache, arthritis and many other diseases are discussed.

There are some wonderful tongue-in-cheek stories. Among these is the tale of the American farmer who, suffering from an invasion of rats, decides to appeal to their sense of fair play. He writes them a civil letter and pins it up in the barn. The note advises them that his crops were short that year, that he could not afford to keep the rats fed throughout the winter, that in the past he had been very kind to them and that, for their own good he thinks they had better leave him now and go to his neighbour's barn where there is more grain than in his.

How Many Miles to Babylon?

JENNIFER JOHNSTON

Despite the fact that possibly more Irishmen died or were wounded or maimed in it than in any other conflict at home or abroad, the First World War barely raises its head above the surface in the landscape of Irish literature. Apart from a few notable contemporaries such as Patrick McGill, Francis Ledwidge and Seán O'Casey, the war or its effects on Irish life hardly rated a mention. By the 1950s it was seen as 'That something or other going on in Europe' while Ireland fought for her independence, and in the run-up to the fiftieth anniversary of the 1916 Rising, it had disappeared off the Irish stage altogether.

Jennifer Johnston's novel *How Many Miles to Babylon?* published in 1974, was something of a shock to the Irish literary and cultural system. Her two previous novels had gained her deserved critical notice but nothing had prepared the Irish public for this powerhouse. It was the first mature expression of that authoritative and sophisticated voice that was to inform the rest of her work and become her trademark.

Born in Dublin in 1930, the daughter of the playwright Denis Johnston and actor Shelah Richards, Jennifer Johnston was educated at Park House School and Trinity College Dublin. She established her reputation during the 1970s, becoming one of Ireland's leading and most consistent novelists, her main theme the isolation suffered by the Ascendancy as their political and social power waned. She developed a particularly spare style of

writing, not wasting a word, earning herself the reputation of being the mistress of the two-word sentence.

In *How Many Miles to Babylon?* Johnston's unique style finds full expression. From the first sentence, the prose is clipped, crisp and informative. We meet Alexander Moore, an officer in the English army who is about to be executed: 'There is no place for speculation or hope, or even dreams. Strangely enough, I think I like it like that.'

He is the only child of the unhappy couple who live in the Big House, who hardly talk to each other while alone but who can be animated and entertaining when in public. He is brought up in a world of long awkward silences, isolated by his over-protective mother from human contact with anyone his own age.

Jerry is the stable hand who 'had a neat facility of keeping out of the way of the horse's hooves and the fists of the more quick-tempered men.' Jerry's feet are bare, Alexander's are covered in black leather and, although they see each other nearly every day, they never speak until Alexander, trying to escape his mother's solicitudes, wanders into the local wood. Suddenly Alexander has a friend, a private and secret friend.

The friendship flourishes but is doomed by the barriers created by their different social backgrounds. The book takes us from the basis of that friendship, their common love of horses, to its final tragic conclusion on the field of Flanders where their deep personal bond triumphs over the brutalisation of the Great War.

An Béal Bocht

Myles na gCopaleen

Sa bhliain 1941 bhí Éire breá sásta léi féin. Bhí a neamhspleáchas aici. Bhí a Bunreacht Caitliceach féin aici. Don chéad uair riamh, bhí a Taoiseach in ann seasamh suas os comhair Príomh-Aire Shasana agus a rá leis go poiblí ar an raidió go raibh a intinn féin aici agus nach raibh suim dá laghad aige a bheith ag troid taobh le Sasana sa gCogadh Mór.

Agus bhí na Gaeltachtaí aici. Seo iad na réigiúin ba mhó a raibh spiorad agus anam na nGael le feiceáil iontu. Ba sna réigiúin seo a bhí an teanga dhúchais agus na hamhráin traidisiúnta beo bríomhar ach ba iad na ceantair ba bhoichte agus ba iargúlta sa tír freisin. Bhí na Gaeltachtaí sách cóngarach, áfach, go raibh daoine sibhialta in ann cuairt a thabhairt orthu uair sa bhliain chun a gcuid Gaeilge a fheabhsú, agus fada go leor ó bhaile gurbh fhéidir dearmad glan a dhéanamh orthu an chuid eile den bhliain. Ní hamháin sin ach ní raibh costas mór i gceist ó thaobh an rialtais de. Dá gcaithfí beagán airgid leo ó am go chéile, bheidís sásta. An rud ba thábhachtaí don tír, iad a choinneáil bocht, salach agus aineolach.

Ait go leor, i dtír a bhí chomh liteartha is a bhí Éire, áit a raibh an oiread sin scríbhneoirí, ní raibh aon chur síos ceart ar na réigiúin áirithe seo. Bhí fear amháin ann, áfach, a rugadh i dTír Eoghain agus a chaith cuid mhaith dá óige i nGaeltacht Thír Chonaill. Bhí cónaí air i mBaile Átha Cliath ag an am seo agus bhain sé clú agus cáil amach dó féin nuair a d'fhoilsigh sé

At Swim Two Birds i 1939. Thuig sé tábhacht na Gaeltachta agus bhí sé in ann cuntas cruinn a scríobh fúithi. Ba é sin Brian Ó Nualláin, nó Flann O'Brien, nó Myles na gCopaleen. D'fhoilsigh sé Bíobla na nGaelteachtaí, *An Béal Bocht*, i 1941. Sa leabhar seo, feictear na Gaeltachtaí eagsúla mar aon réigiún amháin. Dá mbreathnódh laoch an scéil amach tríd an bhfuinneog ar thaobh na láimhe deise dá theach, bhí sé in ann Oileán Thoraí a fheiceáil; dá mbreathnódh sé amach tríd an bhfuinneog ar thaobh na láimhe clé, d'fheicfeadh sé an Blascaod Mór agus bhí sé in ann Inis Mór a fheiceáil amach tríd an doras. Bhí clann thraidisiúnta aige. Ba fhear cneasta a athair cé nár thuig sé cúrsaí an tsaoil go rómhaith. Chaith a mháthair a saol 'ag glanadh amach an tí, ag scuabadh aoileach eallaigh agus muc ó bhéal dorais, ag maistreadh agus ag bleán bó, ag fíodóireacht, ag cardáil olla agus ag casadh an tuirne, ag guí, ag eascainí agus cur síos tinte móra le lán an tí de phrátaí a bhruith in aghaidh lae an ghorta.'

Agus bhí duine eile sa teach, duine riachtanach sa teaghlach traidisiúnta, an seanduine 'cam cromtha a bhí ar mhaide, dhá thrian dá ghniúis agus lán a bhrollaigh gan aon radharc orthu mar go raibh féasóg fhiáin olannliath sa bhealach ann.'

Is aoir den scoth *An Béal Bocht* faoin saol sa Ghaeltacht agus iompar oifigiúil na tíre ina leith. Tá úsáid an-éifeachtach teanga sa leabhar chomh maith le sean-nathanna a bhí i ngnathusáid i 1940 chun fócas a chur ar fhimínteach an Rialtais agus na tíre go ginearálta ó thaobh na Gaeltachta agus na Gaeilge. Críochnaíonn an t-údar gach eachtra leis an abairt: 'Ní bheidh a leithéid ann arís: A mhalairt de scéal atá ann, tá a leithéid ann i gconaí.'

Birchwood

John Banville

In a Banville novel, nothing ever seems to happen. The characters drift on a sea of words with no idea of direction or purpose. The prose with which Banville explores his aesthetic is beguiling and seductive. The Banvillian sentence is almost soporific, numbing the reader with the beauty of its language and rhythm, each word with its own tangible texture, so beautifully and precisely placed that its narrative elements are submerged. It is often remarked that while one would love to write the way Banville does, one wouldn't necessarily like to be the author of his books.

Yet there is something tangible there, something more concrete than a mere indulgence in one's ability to weave beautiful webs of language, and in his second novel *Birchwood*, published in 1973, we are allowed a rare example of the genius of Banville as narrator.

In *Birchwood* we revisit that grand old theme of Irish literature, the 'Big House'. It is set some time during the nineteenth century and our hero, young Gabriel Godkin is the supposed heir of the Big House, Birchwood, in which he was born.

The story is narrated by Gabriel, who relates how his family originally gained possession of the estate from the Lawless family, how his father, an inept landlord, marries into the Lawless family, how his grandparents die in dramatic fashion, the arrival of Aunt Marsha and her son Michael, the encroaching madness of his mother. In fact the whole house seems to be tottering on the verge of bankruptcy, alcoholic delirium and chaos, during which

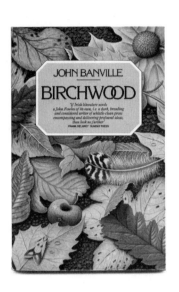

JOHN BANVILLE

BIRCHWOOD

*'If Irish literature needs
a John Fowles of its own, i.e. a dark, brooding
and considered writer of whistle-clean prose
encompassing and delivering profound ideas,
then look no further'*
FRANK DELANEY SUNDAY PRESS

Gabriel makes a disturbing discovery about his own birth:

> And as in this present toil too was the way that day
> in which my fevered brain was working. I went back
> through many years, as many as I could remember,
> gathering fragments of evidence, feeling my way
> around certain discrepancies, retrieving chance words
> let drop and immediately picked up again, collating
> all these scraps that pointed unmistakably, as I now
> saw, to one awesome and abiding fact, namely, that
> somewhere I had a sister, my twin, a lost child. This
> discovery filled me with excitement, but I could not say
> whether the excitement was produced by the cool and
> lucid manner in which I marshalled the evidence or by
> the conclusion which I had reached and that troubled
> me. But a sister! Half of me, somewhere, stolen by the
> circus, or spirited away by an evil aunt, or kidnapped
> by a jealous cousin – and why? A part of me stolen,
> yes, that was a thrilling notion. I was incomplete, and
> would remain so until I found her. All this was real to
> me, and perfectly reasonable.

The second half of the book describes Gabriel's search for
the lost sister and its dénouement is as unexpected and exotic as
Banville's prose in describing it.

Translations

BRIAN FRIEL

When, in 1980, Galway audience took their seats on the hard chairs of the auditorium (the erstwhile basketball court) in Coláiste Iognáid and the curtains opened on the bright new Field Day Theatre Company from Derry and their performance of the first production of Brian Friel's *Translations*, they were far more interested in the locally popular actor Mick Lally who played the leading role of Manus than in the actor who played the minor role of Doalty, one Liam Neeson. Some five years earlier, the same auditorium had hosted the first productions of the fledgling Druid Theatre, in which Lally had played an equally prominent part thus showed that, despite the so-called esteem in which Ireland holds its tradition of drama, two such important events in the history of the modern Irish theatre had to resort to a school's sport hall for a venue.

As they went home that evening, however, the Galway audience was aware that they had been privileged to attend the first production of a work of genius by one of Ireland's leading dramatists.

Born in Omagh, County Tyrone in 1929, Brian Friel was educated in St Columb's in Derry. After a two-year stint in the seminary at Maynooth, he finished his education at St Joseph's College, Belfast and worked as a teacher in Derry until he became a full-time writer in 1960. Initially the author of short stories which appeared in American magazines such as the *New Yorker*,

and of which there were two collections published, *The Saucer of Larks* (1962) and *The Gold in the Sea* (1966), Friel also began to write radio plays for the BBC before the Abbey produced his first stage play, *The Enemy Within,* in 1962. Two years later *Philadelphia Here I Come* confirmed his reputation as a playwright. In 1980 he was a founder member of the Field Day Theatre Company.

The plot of *Translations* is deceptively simple. The action takes place in a hedge school in Friel's fictional Donegal village of Ballybeg, in August 1833. Nearby a detachment of the Royal Engineers has arrived with the intention of making the first ordnance survey of the area.

For the purposes of the English-speaking government, all the local Irish names in this Irish-speaking area have to be rendered into English. Here is the kernel of the play. The effect of the language change on the community is traumatic. It is further complicated by the Latin pedantry of hedge-schoolmaster Hugh and his sidekick Jimmy Jack Cassie.

As the play progresses the ramifications of the language change for the small community become increasingly complex with both comic and tragic results. There is a number of wonderful scenes where two characters are using two different languages although both are speaking in English, where the genius of Friel's writing ensures that the audience instinctively knows which language each character is using and when.

In *Translations* Friel strips people bare of their pretensions and leaves them struggling to find a true common language in which they can express their fears and aspirations.

Connemara Journal

ETHEL MANNIN

After lunch I spend some time in a second-hand bookshop where I spend literally my last shilling – I have my return bus fare carefully put aside – on a shabby Keats with some incredibly fatuous and pointless illustrations. I look through a two-volume edition of Mark Twain's *Autobiography* and I am interested in a facsimile of a portion of the manuscript in which he says he 'writes from the grave' and that only from there can a man write fearlessly... I leave the shop pondering these words.

This must have been the first time that our bookshop featured in a book, six years after it opened its doors,. You can be sure that the shilling Ethel Mannin spent there on her day trip to Galway from her Connemara retreat was most gratefully received: the shop was relatively quiet in those early years.

Born in England in 1900 of Irish parents, Ethel Mannin was the author of a hundred books, nearly half of which were fiction. Although a fiercely independent lady of what would at the time be considered liberal views, questionable morals and dangerous political leanings, her most popular book, as far as Ireland was concerned, was *Late Have I Loved Thee*, in which an Englishman converts to Catholicism and later joins the Jesuits.

Mannin enjoyed a close relationship with W.B. Yeats towards

ETHEL MANNIN'S

Connemara

Journal

the end of his life. She corresponded with Flann O'Brien and was instrumental in having Francis Stuart released from prison after the Second World War.

During the 1940s, Mannin maintained a cottage close to Clifden and would retreat there for months at a time to recover from war-weariness and nourish her own spiritual well-being. *Connemara Journal* is a record of these retreats.

Illustrated with wood engravings by Elizabeth Rivers, the book is written in a down-to-earth style which mirrors the pragmatic approach the author adopted in making comfortable her rough abode. She was acutely aware of the locals' opinion of her ('They all knew I was the mad English writer who had taken a cottage in the wilds of Connemara, was known to have had two husbands and reputed, God help me, to have had nine.') but gained their respect by working as hard as themselves.

As she struggles daily with the inhospitable terrain and the inclement weather, there grows in her a love and respect for the landscape and the people, though this often finds laconic expression: 'What can you do about a country in which it rains even when the sun shines? What can you do, indeed, except admire the rainbows and be thankful.'

Over time, she reaches a level of spiritual calm that allows her to survey the devastation and acrid landscape of post-war Europe with detachment. At the end of the book we find her sadly but firmly shutting the doors of her cottage: 'Tomorrow I must close the shutters, but O hills, O bogs, O shinning waters, O small white house along the boreen, I shall come back, God willing, *I shall came back.*'

In Connemara Journal Ethel Mannin sounds an authentic note of landscape and spiritual rejuvenation, avoiding sentimentality and with a sense of humour that delights and enlightens.

The Unfortunate Fursey

Mervyn Wall

The Unfortunate Fursey requires complete suspension of disbelief. Otherwise the reader will feel lost in a world of indulgent fantasy and will lose interest, missing the point of the book. The first sentence is indication enough of this:

> It is related in the annals that, for the first four centuries after its foundation by the blessed Kieran the monastic settlement of Clonmacnoise enjoyed a singular immunity from the visitations of imps and ghouls, night fiends, goblins and all sorts of hellish phantoms which not unseldom appear to men.

Needless to say, these comments are the prelude to a concerted attack on the holy settlement by disembodied spirits, lemuses, fauns, cacodemons, evil spirits in the form of beautiful harlots, pale bleeding wraiths, hydras, scorpions, ounces, pards and serpents – and the Prince of Darkness himself.

But this massive assault on the saintliness of the hallowed ground is of no avail, so the doyens of evil turn their combined and powerful attentions on the weakest member of the community, Brother Fursey, who 'possessed the virtue of Holy Simplicity in such a degree that he was considered unfit for any work other than paring edible roots in the monastery kitchen.'

The Unfortunate Fursey was published in 1946 by the Pilot

Press. It was written by Mervyn Wall (1908-97) who was born in Dublin to a propertied professional family. He was educated in Belvedere College from where, at fourteen, he was taken by his father and sent to Bonn. There he was put under the tutelage of a Jesuit priest and his family to learn music and painting, subjects in which he had no interest and for which he had no talent. However his time there gave him a respect for German culture and he later returned to Germany on a holiday in the 1930s. There he attended one of Hitler's rallies and found it a frightening experience.

He joined the Irish civil service in 1934 and worked there for most of his career, serving as Programme Assistant to Radio Éireann from 1948 to 1957 and Secretary to the Arts Council in 1957. He is the author of several plays, short stories and novels and is best remembered for *The Unfortunate Fursey*.

As the book progresses and Brother Fursey finds himself expelled from Clonmacnoise, the reader is drawn more and more into what is a savage satire on the Ireland of the 1940s. Wall's main targets are the Church, the politicians and the civil service. However, the main target is undoubtedly the hypocrisy and arrogance of the Church. We meet Father Furiosus who 'was a man of powerful frame, and you had but to observe the great knotted fist clutching a heavy blackthorn stick to have it borne in powerfully upon you that the Church Militant was no empty phrase.'

We meet the misogynist Bishop Flanagan who has great difficulty in understanding why God created women: 'I assume with a blind faith that they are in the world for the trial and affliction of man, that his entry into another sphere may be the more glorious for the temptations he has successfully withstood in this.' The action of the book is fast and furious, becoming more and more ludicrous until the Devil cuts a deal with the bishops.

The Collected Poems

W.B. Yeats

On a dark wet morning in 1948, a young woman and a much younger boy were cycling into Galway along the Grattan Road, watching with great interest a ship round the lighthouse on Mutton Island and head for home. They arrived at the harbour in time to see the ship dock and watched with some awe as its precious cargo was ceremoniously landed. While they had a sense of occasion, few others had. Ireland's leading poet, William Butler Yeats, would have been most displeased at the dismal crowd that showed up at Galway dock that morning to welcome him home to his native soil before he began his final journey to the grave under Ben Bulben.

That young woman was Mother and her much younger companion was Uncle Ivor.

William Butler Yeats made major contributions not just to poetry but to Irish drama, folklore, politics, philosophy and culture. However it is specifically as a poet that he is best remembered, and perhaps the best way to understand the full extent of his contribution to poetry is to read through, at least once, *The Collected Poems*.

W.B. Yeats (1865-1939) was born in Sligo and spent his youth there and in Dublin and London. He was introduced to Irish literature by George Russell and John O'Leary and in June 1892 he founded the National Literary Society which not only engendered an Irish literary revival but also helped to create

conditions for the revival of the Irish language under the auspices of the Gaelic League in 1893. In 1897, along with Lady Gregory of Coole Park and neighbour Edward Martyn, he founded the Abbey Theatre.

His first volume *Mosada: A Dramatic Poem* was published in 1886, his first full collection *Crossways* in 1889. From then until his death, he published several volumes of lyrical poetry as well as longer narrative and dramatic poems, plays, volumes of essays and memoirs, not to mention the anthologies of stories and poetry he edited.

Almost every collection of Yeats includes lines that are so well known as to have become something of a cliché. For example in *Crossways* we have the exquisite love song 'Down By the Salley Gardens', and also 'The Stolen Child'.

The Rose (1893) contained his most popular poem 'The Lake Isle of Inishfree'. It also contained these memorable lines:

> When you are old and full of sleep
> And nodding by the fire, take down this book
> And slowly read and dream of the soft look
> Your eyes had once and of their shadows deep.

There is much more: 'Romantic Ireland's is dead and gone', 'Tread softly for you tread on my dreams' and Mother's favourite lines, from 'In Memory of Eva Gore-Booth and Con Markievicz':

> Two girls in silk kimonos, both
> Beautiful, one a gazelle.

The Guards

KEN BRUEN

One evening, twenty-odd years ago, at an unusually late hour for us, herself and myself were in the Galway Arms, a good hostelry to be in, at the top of Dominick Street. The door opened and a thin, slightly edgy young man walked in carrying a basket of books, one copy of which he left on each table. My first reaction was that he was of an unusual religious or political persuasion and trying to spread the gospel. My second was that it was a question of a charitable donation for himself and I was inclined to leave the book where it was. However my bookseller curiosity got the better of me and I was perusing the pages when the thin young man returned.

'Did you write this?'

'I did'

'Can you call in and see me in the morning?'

'And who the fuck are you?'

'Des Kenny'

'Jaysus, I'll be there at ten.'

And so he was, making us one of the first bookshops, certainly the first in Ireland, to stock Ken Bruen.

Born in Galway in 1951, Ken Bruen is the quintessential Galwegian. He was educated there and at Trinity College Dublin, where he took a doctorate in metaphysics. His itchy feet took him on a twenty-five-year trip around the world where he mostly taught English, re-educated himself and spent six months as the

unwilling guest of a caring Brazilian government. Returning to London, he continued to teach English.

When he found himself in an East London school trying to teach children poetry in a language they didn't understand, he began to write novels in a language they did, introducing literary figures into the text; hence you have such titles as *Her Last Call to Louis MacNiece* and *Rilke on Black*. Thanks to the vision and money of publisher Jim Driver these books saw the light of day.

Sadly, Jim was no distributor and, because the books were so much on the edge and raw, the public remained largely unaware of them. In an attempt to increase his audience Bruen hawked the books himself from pub to pub.

When in 2001, Brandon published his eleventh book – the first in the Jack Taylor series – Bruen became an overnight success.

Jack Taylor could be Mike Hammer or Philip Marlowe, or any one of a thousand other hard-nosed alcoholic ex-cops scrounging around for a sense of self-respect and life-meaning, still doing the odd investigation usually against the run of play: but with a Galway twist.

Bruen's prose is fast and uncompromising, with savage twists of humour intermingled with surprising moments of kindness.

Ken Bruen's *The Guards* breaks new ground and is a harbinger of a whole new tradition in Irish writing, a tradition which openly addresses some home truths about the Ireland we live in. Purportedly an easy read, it is a book of many levels, a fact that is perhaps best enshrined in one of its epigrams:

> I miss a lot of things
> but most of all
> I miss myself.

The Plough and the Stars

SEÁN O'CASEY

Seán O'Casey was born at 85 Lower Dorset Street on 30 March 1880, of lower-class Protestant stock living in a predominantly Catholic area. He grew up in poverty, the youngest of thirteen children, eight of which did not survive childhood. His father Michael earned a modest salary as a clerk and barely managed to keep the household going and he died suddenly, reducing the family to the penury and hardship of the Dublin tenements. This upbringing largely provided the backdrop for Sean O'Casey's three better-known plays, among them *The Plough and the Stars*.

Forced to work at the age of fourteen due to lack of money (and a painful eye disease which prevented him from pursuing formal education), O'Casey was employed in a variety of manual jobs, most of them on the Great Northern Railway. He lived with his mother, who constantly encouraged him to read and educate himself further, until she died in 1918. During the same period, O'Casey involved himself in several movements such as the Gaelic League, the Gaelic Athletic Association and the Irish Republican Brotherhood. Most significantly however, he joined Jim Larkin's Irish Transport and General Workers Union, becoming secretary of its political wing. He left this in 1914 because the union was veering towards nationalism and away from socialism.

O'Casey's first writings were essays and other pieces of journalism for the *Irish Worker* and similar labour or socialist publications. In 1919, he published *The Story of the Irish Citizen*

and the Stars

By Sean O'Casey

✣

*T*HOSE *who have read Sean O'Casey's two other plays will be eager for* The Plough and the Stars. *His keen dramatic sense and Irish wit are here turned upon the pathos and humor of the Rebellion, Irish nationalism as it appealed to those in Dublin's tenement districts. The naked Irish Republican is here, inflamed by his leader's oratory; the quiet man who wants only to live his life far from danger; and the Socialist who quotes Marx better than he handles a gun. ∴ The woman Luke is oh, so. ∴ Bessie Burgess is an out-and-out Orangy, while Nora would do anything to keep her Jack away from the Citizen Army, and Mrs. Gogan minds everyone's business better than her own. ∴ His characters are typical Irish who, like most of us, never agree with each other so well as when disagreeing with some one else.*

Mr. O'Casey's previous play, Juno and the Paycock, *won the Hawthornden Prize for the best work of imaginative literature produced during the year by a writer under forty. ∴ In awarding the prize it was described as "the most moving and most impressive drama we have seen for ten, it may be twenty, years."*

THE MACMILLAN COMPANY

Army under the pseudonym P. Ó Cathasaigh. A number of his plays were rejected by the Abbey Theatre before *The Shadow of a Gunman* was produced in 1923, the first of a trilogy culminating in the production of *The Plough and the Stars* in 1926.

The Plough and the Stars is set in a Dublin tenement prior to and during the 1916 Rising. Newly married, Nora Clitheroe is trying to make a decent home out of her tenement dwelling but her attempts to break out of the poverty trap engender the jealousy of neighbours, the gossip Mrs. Gogan whose daughter is dying from consumption and Orangewoman Bessie Burgess, whose son is fighting on the fields of France. Nora's husband Jack has recently been disappointed in not being promoted captain to in Irish Citizen Army.

The play opens with Fluther Good repairing the lock to Nora's door. Mrs Gogan accepts a package from Arnott's for Nora, which arouses her curiosity and jealousy. She complains to Fluther that no matter how Nora beautifies herself the wonder will wear off Jack soon. Fluther's reply is a superb example of the quick humour and wonderful language that energises the play:

> I dunno, I dunno. Not wishin' to say anything derogatory, I think it's all a question of location: when a man finds th' wondher of one woman beginnin' to die, it's usually beginnin' to live in another.

The play is a study of the effects the 1916 Rising had on the small tight-knit community of a tenement dwelling. In the character of Bessie Burgess, O'Casey cleverly introduces the shadow of the First World War and the tragedy it caused for the thousands of Irish families whose sons it killed or maimed.

There Was an Ancient House

BENEDICT KIELY

To my relief, he was on the train. He was wont to miss them. The car was parked less than a hundred yards away. He was to open George Campbell's exhibition that evening and, should he meet anyone betwixt train and car, the chances were that the day would be spent in some nearby hostelry with many a good story and song, but no one fit to open an exhibition.

He was carrying a small case and a large hold-all. He was to have with him the bronze head of George Campbell and I presumed it was in the hold-all. I went to pick it up and passed a comment on its weight. A gleam came into his eyes:

'The Dublin porter said something similar in Heuston station and wondered if the mother-in-law was in it. You should have seen his face when I told him that it was the head of George Campbell.'

The anecdote was typical of the man and makes it all the more interesting that he should be the author of the deeply sensitive and moving novel *There Was an Ancient House*.

Born in 1919 in Dromore, County Tyrone, Benedict Kiely was educated by the Christian Brothers in Omagh and spent two years in a Jesuit novitiate in County Laois before moving to Dublin. There he worked as a journalist with the *Irish Press* until 1964, after which he spent a number of years teaching in American universities. The rest of his life was spent as a broadcaster, lecturer and writer in Dublin. Ben Kiely was a superb storyteller, steeped

in the age-old tradition of the *seanchaí*. He died in 2007.

There Was an Ancient House was published in 1955. Based on Kiely's experience in the Jesuit novitiate, it tells the story of thirty novices in their first year in the seminary.

In typical Kiely fashion, we sidle into the story gradually, inching towards its heart as the novelist explores the effect the seminary has on each of the novices. Any individual action, thought or even mannerism is discouraged and it is the slow realisation that they have sacrificed their individual identities that causes them to question the true value of their own vocation. As the year progresses, individual novices begin to 'take their hand from the plough'. After the first departure, there is a general air of depression but the intensity of this diminishes with each successive one. Curiously, celibacy is the least of the problems for the novices:

> I'd like for a break in monastic monotony to peep into a corner where life would be as even as the ticking of an old clock, no regrets for the fleshpots... I'd like to see life again, not drink not jollification, neither excitement nor sin, but quiet people living in an easy world that makes its own rules, needs no bells, no imposed pattern.

By writing with empathy for both the novices and their superiors, Kiely allows us a rare insight into the intense personal debate a man had to undergo before achieving – or not achieving – ordination.

Death and Nightingales

Eugene McCabe

Two men, one a gardener, the other his current employer, a writer, were sitting on the garden wall chatting about this and that and nothing in particular and everything in general. For no reason at all, the gardener suddenly pointed in the direction of what was, in fact, an overgrown path and said: 'They went that way.'

The employer, being a writer, was naturally curious and asked: 'Who went that way?'

For the next hour or so the writer, Eugene McCabe, listened to the tale that was to become the basis for his novel *Death and Nightingales*.

Born in Glasgow of Monaghan stock in 1930, McCabe was educated in Castleknock College and University College Cork. He took over the management of the family farm on the Monaghan/Fermanagh border in 1964. Best recognised as a playwright, his most successful play is *The King of the Castle* (1964). *Victims* (1976), a trilogy for television, remains probably the most powerful dramatic presentation of the horrors of the Ulster conflict. McCabe is also the author of a number of collections of short stories and a children's tale *Cyril*. *Death and Nightingales*, his first stand-alone novel, was published in 1992.

Death and Nightingales is a good old-fashioned historical romance tinged with a curious sharpness. It is set in Fermanagh in the Ireland of 1883 with Parnell at the height of his powers, Percy French touring the country packing them in with his humorous

and romantic ballads and the dark shadow of the 'Invincibles' hanging over the country, a stark reminder that all was not yet settled between the Gael and the Gall.

In the powerful opening sequence we find our heroine, Beth Winters, dreaming of the properties of various poisons. She is awakened by the bawling of a cow and realising there is no one else going to relieve the suffering animal – her father Billy Winters, a wealthy Protestant farmer and landlord is sprawled in a drunken sleep – she arms herself with a canula, a hollow pointed veterinary instrument with a clearing plunger, and goes to the field where she finds the stricken beast. In a determined and decisive manner that would do any self-respecting vet proud, she relieves the animal of the gas trapped in its stomach. The day is her twenty-fifth birthday and she is planning to rob her father that evening.

Except that he is not her father and thereby unfolds a tale of love, an arranged marriage, domestic and personal violent abuse, a savage and fatal accident of a young pregnant woman, treachery and revenge. Couple this with sleeping draughts, midnight trysts, conniving maids, gambling debts and political intrigue and you have all the hallmarks of a historical thriller.

Death and Nightingales is the classical historical novel – of which there are few in the Irish literary canon – based on a folktale. It is written in a sparse, lean and economic prose and has an exceptionally strong narrative line. It is one of the most enjoyable books of its kind.

Dead as Doornails

ANTHONY CRONIN

I remember being assigned to host Benedict Kiely and Anthony Cronin for lunch the day after a book launch. The Olde Malte Restaurant being the nearest, we adjourned there. The two writers were in sparkling form, the revels of the previous night continuing unabated. Towards the end of the meal they got into a mostly friendly debate in relation to some point of Irish history and had reached a sticky point when Kiely, encouraged by Cronin, burst into song. After entertaining us with a verse or two, he stood up and addressed the bemused lunchers: 'That, ladies and gentlemen, was merely to illustrate an historical point.' He sat down to rapturous applause. It was as close as I was ever going to get to the bohemian ambience of the literary circles of Dublin during the 1940s and 1950s, the world so skilfully celebrated in Anthony Cronin's classic memoir *Dead as Doornails*.

Born in 1928 in Wexford, Cronin was educated there and in University College Dublin where he qualified as a barrister. He worked in a legal office for a while, earning seven pounds and three shillings a week, but it was, he writes, 'a state in which I took no pride, indeed I was acutely ashamed of it.' Before long, he had left this work to pursue a career as poet and literary critic.

In *Dead as Doornails*, Cronin records his association with seven men – Ralph Cusack, Brendan Behan, Patrick Kavanagh, Brian O'Nolan (Myles na gCopaleen), Robert Colquhoun, Robert MacBryde and Julian McLaren Ross – from the early

1940s through to the death of Patrick Kavanagh in 1967.

Of them all, Cronin was closest to Behan. The book has a wonderful description of their sojourn in France where they posed as '*deux Irlandais en pélérinage à Rome*,' and tramped Godot-like through the country. Penniless and bedless, our two heroes are facing a rough night sleeping out in Paris when Behan asks Cronin if he would prefer to be a great writer but poor and recognised or a lionised one who was a failure and a fraud:

> With the summer night about us and the lights still on in Maxims and the Tour d'Argent I said I thought one would be better off being the first fellow. After a long pause he said quietly that he was not sure.

Kavanagh, Cronin contends, was like a fish out of water in Dublin. Because his genius was misunderstood, he became a caricature. Knowing his reputation, Cronin expected a yob when he first met him:

> It therefore came as something of a surprise to me…to find that Patrick Kavanagh was a deeply serious man with an intellect which was humorous and agile as well as being profound and apparently incorruptible…On somebody who already admired his work his impact was extraordinary.

Kavanagh and O'Nolan dominate the rest of the book and there is an account of the first Bloomsday celebration in 1954. Written with great humour and total honesty, *Dead as Doornails* is an authentic portrait of a difficult time for creative writers in Ireland. By focusing on their human and spiritual struggles, it enhances our appreciation of their literary achievements.

Cúirt an Mheán-Oiche

BRIAN MERRIMAN

Ba gnáth me ag siúl le ciumhais na habhann
Ar bháinseach úr 's an drúcht go trom,
In aice na gcoillte, i gcoim an tsléibhe,
Gan mhairg, gan mhoill, ar shoilse an lae.
Do ghealadh mo chroí nuair chínn Loch Gréine,
An talamh 's an tír is íor na spéire;
taitneamhacht aoibhinn suíomh na sléibhte
ag bagairt a gcinn thar dhroim a chéile.

Dá mbeadh a fhios againn mar ghasúir scoile go raibh níos
mó i gceist leis an dán seo ná an tírdhreach álainn a chuirtear
i láthair sna chéad línte, déarfainn go mbeadh i bhfad níos mó
suime againn sa dán céanna nuair a bhíomar á fhoghlaim don
Ardteist. Más cuimhin liom i gceart, dúradh linn ag an am nach
raibh sa dán uilig ach na hocht líne sin agus go raibh sé ar cheann
de na dánta ab fhearr a cumadh riamh faoin nádúr. Bhí ár gcuid
múinteoirí ag cur dallamullóg cheart orainn! Bheadh sé spéisiúil
fios a bheith againn céard a bhí ag rith trí intinn Brian Merriman,
a bhí ina mhúinteoir é féin, nuair a chum sé na línte tosaigh sin
den dán fada *Cúirt an Mheán Oíche* i 1780.

Rugadh Brian Merriman i gContae an Chláir thart ar an
mbliain 1747. Is cosúil go raibh sé ina mhúinteoir i scoil scairte
agus go raibh scoil aige sa bhFiacail i 1770. Thóg sé feirm fiche
acra ar cíos. Phós sé i 1790 agus bhog sé go Luimneach go luath

ina dhiaidh sin. Fuair sé bás ansin i 1805.

Possibly one of the most original long poems ever written, *The Midnight Court*, despite being firmly based in the Clare folk tradition, is a perfect composition by any standard. Using, and thereby satirising the traditional poetry Irish format of the aisling (whereby Ireland, in the shape of a beautiful woman, appears to the poet in a dream and complains about the poor state of the country), the poet falls asleep on the shores of Lough Greaney just outside Feakle. He is visited in the dream by an Amazon ('*An Mhásach bholgach tholgach thaibhseach Chamach/ cholgach ghoirgeach ghaibhdeach*') who summons him – or rather drags him – to the court of Queen Aoibheal, the fairy queen of north Munster.

Before the court, the poet, representing the men of Ireland, is accused of not having married despite his middle age. There follows a series of female witnesses who accuse the men, especially the clergy, of remaining celibate or of only marrying old hags for monetary gain. The poet defends himself as best he can but is found guilty. He is about to be severely beaten by the assembled women when he wakes up.

Many years ago, there was a musical adaptation of *The Midnight Court* by Seán Tyrrell, produced by Billy Loughnane, a Feakle solicitor, and performed in a marquee on the shores of Lough Greaney, the very spot where Merriman is said to have composed the poem. A brave venture, so brave that herself and myself decided to go. It was a beautiful summer's evening and as we took our seats the atmosphere was electric. A terrific spectacle but even more interesting was the reaction of the audience. The women hooted and cheered and the men grumbled. Then their turn came and they roared back. The women, however, responded with gusto and when the verdict was passed the guy sitting beside me was thumped several times. I saw at least one handbag swinging.

Michael Joe

WILLIAM COTTER MURRAY

There is, in the popular music industry, a phenomenon called the one-hit wonder: a record that climbs to the top of the charts quickly, stays there for a week or two and then disappears just as quickly, almost totally forgotten. Occasionally though, a one-hit wonder gains itself a special place in the fickle hierarchy of the industry and becomes an all-time classic.

In the Irish book world a book that would have strong claims to such a status is *Michael Joe* by William Cotter Murray. The book was, I believe, first published in the United States in 1965. Since then there has been only one reprint issued by Brandon Press in 1991.

Of the author, William Cotter Murray, virtually nothing is known. He doesn't appear in any reference book, nor does he feature in any discussion relating to the twentieth-century Irish novel. The only information relating to him that has surfaced is the short biographical note that appears on the back cover of the Brandon edition which informs us that he was born in Milltown Malbay County Clare in 1942. He emigrated to the United States in 1949. After military service in the Korean War, he joined a writer's workshop in Iowa in 1956. In 1970 he was appointed to the English Department of the University of Iowa.

Both the author and the book deserve a lot more attention than these sketchy notes. If ever a novel defined village life in the rural Ireland of the 1930s, then this is it.

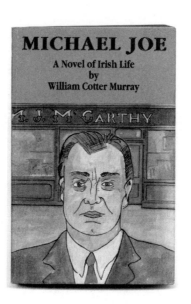

In the first three paragraphs, a classic example of direct, economical informative writing, the author fills us in completely on Michael Joe's family background and sets the tone for the book. Over the next few pages, Murray develops the character of his hero (and more especially his mother's possessiveness), and then introduces the femme fatale.

Coming home suddenly from England, Nell Cullen brings with her an aura of sophistication and mystery that waken in our hero feelings hitherto unknown to him but she rejects his clumsy approaches. This engenders a whole series of personal crises for Michael Joe but he lacks the self knowledge and social control to handle them properly. All his recognised props, while giving him a local popularity, eventually fail him.

The book offers an in-depth canvas of village life in the rural Ireland of the 1930s. In the character of Canon Lyons we have the all-powerful parish priest. Next on the social ladder are the bank managers, followed by their clerks, who are followed in turn by the doctors, merchants, shopkeepers and publicans. Below them is a general class of labourers and loafers and then the farmers, living in the country, seen almost as a race apart.

In the character of Michael Joe himself, William Cotter Murray has given us the classic 'Street Angel, House Devil'.

Despite the lack of attention it has received, this book is a unique record of the realities of life in the rural society of an Ireland trying desperately to define its own identity.

The Collected Poems

PATRICK KAVANAGH

By all accounts, Patrick Kavanagh did not look like your average poet. A tall lumbering man with a heavy step and a deep growling voice, he was more the thick ignorant culchie with boots covered in cow dung whose concerns in life centred around the milk yield of his cattle, the price of potatoes and the possibility that Monaghan might reach the Ulster final. Politics were essentially local, religion pragmatic, but poetry! That was for them that had their heads stuck in 'thim useless books that never put spuds on the table or sold cattle at a fair'.

There is, of course, the possibility that it was this very closeness to the soil, the understanding he had of the seasons, the earth's power of regeneration, the empathy he had for the creatures of the field, the rawness of the life he had known growing up on a Monaghan farm during the 1910s and 1920s that gave his poetry its authentic voice, so that when he did write verse, it struck a deep chord within the heart and soul of the Irish. Or maybe it was the sheer genius of the man.

Kavanagh was born in 1904. His father was a cobbler and a subsistence farmer in the parish of Inniskeen, County Monaghan. With the increasing popularity of 'shop shoes', the cobbling trade failed and the family was reared on the small farm.

Kavanagh's formal schooling ended at thirteen but he continued his education by reading everything he could lay hands on. Almost immediately he started to 'dabble in verse' but it took

nearly a decade before his talent was recognised when George Russell printed three of his poems in the *Irish Statesman*. His first collection was published in 1936, which was quickly followed by his autobiography *The Green Fool*. In 1939, he moved to Dublin and lived there until his death in 1967.

The rough physical presence of Kavanagh belied the extra-ordinary lyricism and intense spirituality of his verse. Like that of all great poets, his work constantly surprises. He was, to a large extent, the champion of poor farmers, expressing in verse the harsh realities and loneliness of their existence, debunking the romantic myths of the pastoral life: their adherence to a sentimental nationalism and triumphalist Catholicism. He keenly felt society's rejection of his genius, a feeling greatly exacerbated by the losses he suffered in two infamous libel cases. Thereafter he sank deeper into alcoholism.

Revisiting his *Collected Poems* is like taking a deep, refreshing breath of clear air. It is a journey of constant discovery, full of new turnings and hitherto hidden byways. In a curious way, the poetry always seems to match the reader's moods and mirror his or her feelings and aspirations. An essential part of Kavanagh's charm is his ironic self-deprecation as a poet:

> I am like a monk
> In a grey cell
> Copying out my soul's
> Queer miracle
> I would be a blue bottle
> Or a house-fly
> And let the monk, the task
> In darkness lie.

Ireland is extremely lucky that, in the poet Patrick Kavanagh, they have the proverbial fly on the wall of life's vicissitudes.

The Farm by Lough Gur

Mary Carbery

The Farm by Lough Gur has strong claims to be the classic Irish pastoral idyll. Mary Toulmin, an Englishwoman, visited Ireland, fell in love and married Lord Carbery of Castle Freke. In the summer of 1904, she was trying to source the words of a lost song in Bruff, County Limerick, where the song was said to have been born. Mary Fogarty welcomed her and regaled her visitor with stories of the notable banshee Áine and her brother Fer Fí the dwarf, tales of faeries in the hollow hills and a drowned city in the Enchanted Lake, as Lough Gur was called.

In 1935, when Mary Carbery asked her friend if she could write down her recollections, Mary Fogarty, now an old lady, produced page after page of handwritten memoirs which Carbery then wove into a sustained narrative and in 1937 *The Farm by Lough Gur* was published for the first time. It has known many reprints since then.

> There is a hill in the county Limerick called Knockfennel whose southern slopes fall steeply into Lough Gur. On a green ridge above the lake stands an old farmhouse where I was born on the twenty-ninth of May, 1858.

Thus begins the story of a tightly-knit Utopian community in the latter half of the nineteenth century. Dominated by the O'Brien family, their son and four daughters, the community

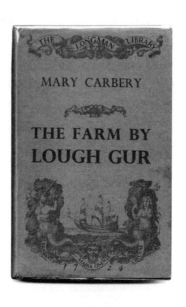

THE LONGMAN LIBRARY

MARY CARBERY

THE FARM BY
LOUGH GUR

is largely self-sufficient and self-contained. John and Anne O'Brien, Mary Fogarty's parents, are enlightened, fairly well-to-do farmers who have a sense of humanity and justice. Their farm is run like clockwork: everybody rising at 4 am, specific tasks and chores being executed in an orderly fashion throughout the day until everybody eventually retires at 9 pm. There is also a strong adherence to daily devotional practices such as the Angelus and the Rosary. While everybody is worked hard, nobody is harshly treated or left in want.

Unusual, if not unique in this rural Irish homestead is a great love of books and literature. There are many references to the poetry of Keats and Byron while the prose of Dickens and Thackeray is frequently invoked. This love of books is not universally shared, 'for cousin Julia exclaimed, "Books are the invention of sinful men! If Almighty God had approved of books He would not have created worms to destroy them."'

The sensitive narrative brings into positive relief the ongoing tension between pagan superstition and contemporary Catholic practices, especially during the May Eve and Hallowe'en celebrations. There are many fascinating visitors to the farm such as 'Me John', 'Billy the Clerk', 'Maggy the Eels' and 'Twomey, whose wife was glad to beat him on Sunday night in return for the beating he gave her on Saturday...'

The Farm by Lough Gur is a wondrous folk biography describing an existence that is no longer possible in today's world. It is also a testament to the strong role played by women in building the social structures that sustain the Ireland of today.

No Time for Work

GEORGE RYAN

One Saturday morning, quite a number of years ago, a rather dishevelled man came into the shop and asked me if he could have a word with me quietly. Wondering what the approach for the 'loan' would be, I brought him to a quieter part of the shop. He was a writer, he told me – aren't we all, I thought – and then, to my surprise, he pulled from his pockets three black-covered paperbacks with the intriguing titles *No Time for Work*, *Vexed at his Own Funeral* and *Time For a Smile*.

He told me his name was George Ryan and was much better known as the *Irish Times* bridge correspondent. In actual fact, he was the author of the smallest bestseller in Irish publishing history, the miniscule *Bones of Bridge*. In another life, he had been a teacher but also was one of those unfortunates who had an inordinate fondness for drink. This 'inordinate fondness' was so strong that he found himself without a job having been through fourteen headmasters, seventeen parish priests and twenty-eight inspectors. Having survived the alcohol, and achieved some respectability (although you might have some difficulty in appreciating this given his appearance on that first Saturday), he decided to cash in on his erstwhile experiences and write the three books.

Somewhat mesmerised by this rather original approach, not to mention the uniqueness of the story, I took ten copies of all three. Reading them later, I realised I had three classics of outrageous

comedy on my hands. Indeed, the books quickly took on a cult status and within a couple of months, Ryan had sold over twenty thousand copies of his books, this at a time when publishers were struggling to sell more than three thousand copies of even the most popular titles.

The books sold out but, some years later, Ryan needed a new car. He looked at his three literary babies and decided they needed dressing up a bit. He incorporated all three of them into one volume, felt the result was much better and in 1979 published the final *No Time for Work*. Within a month, he had sold enough copies to buy the car. In the sample copy he sent me he wrote the following:

> This here is the fourth and final version of my alleged fictional life. In all I've sold 27,500 copies. I had been a teacher who retired four times. Occasionally, I was asked why I gave up the job. My standard reply was that it was interfering with my drinking. My last post was in Straffan, County Kildare. While there I wrote the first edition of *No Time for Work*. Most of the parents in the village bought the book. Some of those, irate and horrified at the contents of my 'autobiography', armed with the book approached the principal Jack Hennigan seeking reassurance. Tongue-in-cheek he opted not to mollify them. One distraught mother asked Jack if I was as bad as portrayed in the novel. He replied 'Much worse! You don't know what I have to put up with.'

Hurrish

Emily Lawless

In the context of the Irish book world, the novel *Hurrish* by Emily Lawless is a curious publication. First published in 1886, it was praised by Gladstone for the light it threw on the relationship between the Irish tenant farmer and English law. The political stance taken by the book is fascinating in that, while being hostile to the Irish Land League (she was a member of a strong Ascendancy family), Emily Lawless also recognised the injustices perpetrated by the status quo and the members of her own class on the Irish tenant farmer.

The book is also significant in its celebration of the Burren countryside and the classical style used by the author to do this. When you have read a sentence written by Emily Lawless describing the topography and the beauty of the Clare landscape, you will know you will have read a perfectly constructed sentence written in the style reminiscent of the classic Victorian essay and so beloved of the English teachers in our schools of yore.

Emily Lawless, eldest daughter of the wealthy landlord Lord Cloncurry, was born in 1845, at Lyons Castle, County Kildare. Her mother was a Kirwan from Castlehackett, County Galway, and she spent half her youth there. She was educated in England.

Although she considered herself to be patriotic, her views on Irish politics did not please nationalists. Amongst other things, she did not believe that Ireland was ready for self-government and believed the Home Rule movement to be a political folly.

CLASSIC · IRISH · NOVELS

HURRISH

Emily
Lawless

with an introduction by
VAL MULKERNS

She wrote a number of novels, most of them historical romances, the last of them *The Races of Castlebar* being written in collaboration with Shan Bullock and published in 1914, the year after her death. Although critical of her monograph on Maria Edgeworth, W.B. Yeats listed two of her titles among his best Irish books, one of them being *Hurrish*.

Subtitled 'A Study', *Hurrish* was first published in 1886 and was Lawless's first novel with an Irish theme. Using the arid, yet variable Burren countryside as her background, the book centres on a young, comfortable and locally popular farmer Horatio O'Brien, known as Hurrish, and the rural community he lives in. Other principal characters include his landlord, the benevolent but troubled Major Pierce O'Brien, and the evilly disturbed and vindictive Mat Brady, whose personal hatred for Hurrish knows no bounds.

With infinite care, Lawless introduces the reader to her cast of characters, who would have been equally at home in a work by Charles Dickens or George Eliot. In Hurrish's household, there is his mother suffused with hatred for England, Ally Sheehan, his orphaned niece who greatly resembles the Dickens character Little Nell, and his own three children. His wife is dead.

As the story begins, our benevolent landlord is forced to lease a farm of land that borders Hurrish's own holding. The prime bidder is Mat Brady, who wants the farm solely for the purpose of inflicting pain and suffering on his neighbour. Despite advice from all sides, the Major leases the farm to Brady and the scene is set . . .

The Tailor and Ansty

ERIC CROSS

Published in 1942, and written by Newry-born Eric Cross (1905-1980), the book *The Tailor and Ansty* became famous for all the wrong reasons. It was banned for being 'in its general tendency indecent'. There was nothing unusual in that. Since the Censorship of Publications Act had been enacted in 1929, it was almost normal for good books to be banned. The standing joke was that you were not deemed to be a writer of worth unless you has at least one book banned – although, of course, this did not diminish the author's personal pain – and the journal *Analecta Hibernica* recently published the journal of a censor written during the early 1950s in which he stated that out of 1274 books read in one year (a major feat in itself) he banned 996.

Most of the bannings went unnoticed (except by the author) and it looked as if the same was going to happen *The Tailor and Ansty*. However, there was some concern about the effects it would have on the subjects of the book, an elderly tailor named Timothy Buckley and his wife Ansty (Anastasia) who lived in a tiny cottage on the mountain road up to Gougane Barra.

In the stultifying atmosphere of the Ireland of the day, scarcely anyone could voice their objections to the banning, but one man, a Protestant landlord, Sir John Keane, did. He tabled a motion in the Irish Senate condemning the Censorship Board. The resultant four-day debate held during 1943 is one of the lowest points in the history of Dáil Éireann, eliciting from Frank

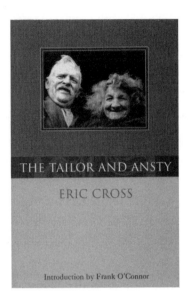

THE TAILOR AND ANSTY

ERIC CROSS

Introduction by Frank O'Connor

O'Connor the statement that 'Reading it is like a long slow swim through a sewage bed.'

The personal fallout for Tim Buckley and his wife was savage and when we watch some of the censorious excesses committed by foreign cultures on their own people today we should remember that similar acts of barbarism were committed in our name just over sixty years ago.

All of this took away from the book, and more's the pity. Reading it now, when thankfully the Censorship Board has almost disappeared from human memory, is like revisiting an old friend one has not seen in years, discovering riches there far more valuable than memory would have them.

'In the townland of Garrynapeaka, in the district of Inchigeela, in the parish of Iveleary, in the barony of West Muskery, in the county of Cork, in the province of Munster' – as he magniloquently styles his address, lives the Tailor. Here is the Tailor's and Ansty's universe and everything is seen in the context of its realities.

The tailor's imagination, much in the style of the old *seanchaí*, with Ansty as the perfect foil, may take us to the four corners of the earth and beyond. But then the world's a quare place entirely and the local parish is a rock of common sense.

The Tailor and Ansty is an immensely cheerful book. Bristling with laughter and good humour, it is full of folk wisdom based on common sense but always tinged with a touch of wonder. For any jaded palate, it is an amazingly refreshing read.

A Goat's Song

DERMOT HEALY

Dermot Healy is one of those writers who fit into whatever landscape they encounter. Whether it is the flat Sunday afternoon of the Irish midlands, the stony windswept shores of the west, the dour austerity of the phlegmatic north, he makes the landscape his natural habitat. Born in 1947 in Finea, County Westmeath, the enigmatic Healy is the only writer on record who, as his own memoir *The Bend for Home* would have it, was born in the wrong bed.

Novelist, short story writer, playwright, poet, essayist, journalist, screenwriter, Healy is comfortable in all of these genres. For more than two decades he was the torch-bearer of Irish literature across the area known officially as the mid-west, being the founder and editor of two of the better journals to grace the Irish literary scene, *The Drumlin* and *Force 10*. His first collection of short stories, *Banished Misfortune,* was published in 1982. He won two Hennessy awards and his memoir *The Bend for Home* contains one of the most devoted and tender descriptions of caring for a senile and incontinent parent that exists in any literature.

A Goat's Song, published in 1994, is possibly his most accomplished work. Purportedly a love story, *A Goat's Song*, like all books of its calibre, is much more than that.

The novel opens with the sentence 'The bad times were over at last.' Jack Ferris, playwright and alcoholic, picks up a letter from the floor of his damp hall which confuses him. 'The letter he had

been expecting would have told him that the relationship was really over. Instead this brief tender missal of love has arrived.' The letter holds the aspiration that resounds throughout the book: 'Let's grow old and sober together.'

Whereas Jack Ferris comes from a loose Catholic west of Ireland background, Catherine Adams, the writer of the letter, is a strict Northern Presbyterian. Her rejection of Ferris sends him into an alcoholic spin which ends in a mental hospital. After treatment, working on a fishing trawler aids his recovery.

As Ferris faces his demons, Healy opens the curtains on Catherine's background – a restrictive Ulster Presbyterian society, where we meet one of the more extraordinary characters of Irish fiction: her father John Adams, a failed preacher who joins the RUC. His whole world is overturned when, during a Derry civil rights march in 1968, he is caught on television swinging a baton at a defenceless marcher. He becomes reclusive and finally seeks refuge by retiring to the west of Ireland.

When *A Goat's Song* was written, the two cultural traditions that exist in the country were politically polarised. That impasse has been largely resolved, but now there are other tensions, cultural and personal, which need to be accepted for what they are. *A Goat's Song* acknowledges this and opens our minds to the fact that the possibility of a better future depends solely on ourselves.

Dhá Scéal/Two Stories

MÁIRTÍN Ó CADHAIN

The Irish language is Ireland's cultural volcano. Most of the time it rumbles, hidden, beneath the surface, a power-house of Ireland's rich indigenous language and culture, reminding us that the language we buy our bread in and the foreign culture we have adopted are not really our own.

There are many gems of Irish literature lost to the general public and many writers' work is largely unknown by the people most in need of it. One such writer is that colossus of Irish literature, the man who was most relentless in describing the drudging poverty of the people of Connemara, particularly the hardship suffered by the women who lived through it, the man from Cnocán Glas in Cois Fharraige, Conamara: Máirtín Ó Cadhain.

Born in 1906, Ó Cadhain was to become the greatest writer in the Irish language of the twentieth century. An unrepentant socialist and republican, he was interned in the Curragh during the Second World War, and it was at this time he developed the narrative style which became his trademark. He was appointed Professor of Modern Irish in Trinity College Dublin the year before he died, in 1970.

Sadly, Ó Cadhain's work remains inaccessible to all but a small audience. Ó Cadhain explores the rich texture of the Irish language and because of this uncompromising approach the full glory and subtlety of his text is beyond the comprehension of all but the few. Many of the words used are particular to Cois

Fharraige and the sentence structures are not to be found in any standard grammar or taught in any of our classrooms.

Strangely, his work has rarely been translated, his masterpiece *Cré na Cille* never. There was, apparently, an English version ready to go to press about twenty years ago in San Francisco, but it wasn't published. Poolbeg Press published an excellent collection of his short stories in 1981 with the title *The Road to Bright City*.

Almost nothing else has been published in anything but the original. To celebrate the centenary of Ó Cadhain's birth, Arlen House, along with Cló Iar Chonnachta and Cúirt '06 published a volume which goes some way to fill the gap.

Entitled *Dhá Scéal/Two Stories*, it is a bilingual printing of two of Ó Cadhain's stories 'Ciumhas an Chriathraigh', ('The Edge of the Bog') and 'An Stráinséar', ('The Stranger'). The strength and power of Ó Cadhain's original text is such that it took the combined talents of three translators, Louis de Paor, Lochlainn Ó Tuairisg and Mike McCormack, to render it into a comparable English.

Their efforts, however, were hugely successful and the resultant volume is a joy to hold and to read. To begin with there is the inherent quality of the stories themselves. From the first sentence we are on a different linguistic and cultural plateau. This allows those few who are able to fully comprehend the subtleties within a new chance to indulge themselves in the feast of language. It allows others of us who have some knowledge of Irish a rare chance to taste the full glory of the language. And it allows those for whom Irish is a foreign language a chance to read the work of Ireland's best-kept literary secret.

In the Wake of the Bagger

JACK HARTE

Some time during the year 2006 a novel arrived in the post. On its cover was the bold announcement that it had been commissioned by Sligo County Council. The book had the curious title of *In the Wake of the Bagger*, and the only thing to recommend it was the name of the author, Jack Harte. Many years before, the poet and publisher John F. Deane had introduced me to this man's work and it had been a positive reading experience. This was his first novel.

The first chapter fulfils that early promise. You are reminded what it is to watch a horse and plough 'opening the soil in a green field at the butt end of winter and to watch the birds gather in flocks and jostle for the rich pickings left behind.' The bagger is a bit like that 'as it caterpillared out on a midlands bog all iron bulk and cautious purpose, brandishing tooth and blade, tearing open the spring bog with its shaft of knife sharp buckets.' Then comes the legend of the book:

> And we followed in the wake of the bagger, like hungry sea birds. From Kerry and Donegal we flocked, from Clare and Mayo, all the lean counties along the west coast of Ireland. And by summer we were scattered out across the turf bank in clutches and clusters, picking sustenance from the excretions of the bagger, rejoicing in our victory over want, making the earth our own.

There is little biographical detail relating to Jack Harte, save that he was born in Easkey, County Sligo, grew up in Lanesboro, County Longford and lives in Dublin. Yet in his novel he offers us a unique insight into an almost forgotten but nonetheless significant part of Ireland's modern social history.

The novel tells the story of a Sligo family called O'Dowd whose father, a blacksmith, is made redundant by advances in technology. He is forced to migrate to the Irish midlands where the massive peat bogs are being commercially exploited for the first time and where there is almost guaranteed employment. The book's narrator is O'Dowd's eldest son, Robbie.

Despite its element of autobiography, this is a stand-alone novel dealing with a strong sense of cultural and physical loss. Many scenes and stories are tinged with magic, some with a tremendous sense of self-irony. The most touching narration of all is the story of the unbaptised baby Angela's death days after her birth. According to the mores of the time, the infant had to be buried in a killeen, a piece of unhallowed ground.

The passage describing the search for the killeen is as close to harrowing as exists in Irish literature. Eventually the possibility of using the Protestant graveyard is voiced, 'Apparently they have no problem with these babies being buried in their consecrated ground. They seem to be more civilised about it than our lot.' Nonetheless the baby had to be buried under cover of darkness.

Zoli

Colum McCann

Recently, Andrew Herkovic, one of our Book Club customers, sent us this letter from Stanford University:

> Started Colum McCann's *Zoli* yesterday – it's already ruined one night's sleep. Did you know that some of the story takes place within fifteen or twenty miles of where my father grew up? I went there once in 1962 with him and his sister. We stayed a few days at an old and grand spa hotel in the Tatra mountains. One day we hired a car for an excursion. They had the driver stop the car in what seemed to me the middle of nowhere. We got out and they pointed to a group of farm buildings several fields – maybe half a mile – away on a hillside, but would go no closer for fear of being recognised. No further explanation was offered. The house in which my father was born, I was told was the one with the distinctive colour roof. Then we went back to the hotel and eventually to Prague, city of ingenuous clocks, golems, defenestrations, tombstones of vaporised ghettos and honour guards with AK-47s. So what I want to know is, what the hell is an Irishman living in New York doing writing a book about Slovakia during the war?

Perhaps the only way to answer that question is to say that Colum McCann is one of the first modern writers with enough skill and self-belief to tackle non-Irish themes and explore them fully. He is not the first writer to do so – Francis Stuart, Aidan Higgins and J.G. Farrell jump to mind – but all of them had some experience of the world of their novels. McCann had none.

Colum McCann has created quite a reputation for himself. His first collection of short stories, *Fishing the Sloe Black River,* sold well and a couple of novels followed which established him as an up-and-coming writer. His novel *Dancer* – a fictional biography of the Russian dancer Nureyev – never got the recognition it deserved. The opening scenes, set in Russia at the end of the Second World War, are quite remarkable.

Zoli is a magnificent piece of work. Its two most remarkable aspects are the atmosphere of the book and the insights it affords us into the daily lives of the Romany gypsies as the Second World War threatened to obliterate them. These insights belie any romantic notions we may have about the gypsies. On the contrary, they demonstrate the harsh social and personal disciplines under which they had to live in order to survive.

There are several different levels to the book and Andrew Herkovic's question is not, perhaps, so surprising. In a curious way it underpins the traumatic effect the Second World War had on Europe, an effect so deep that, sixty years later, a librarian in California should wonder why an Irishman living in New York would write about the society of his Slovakian father.

The Country Girls

EDNA O'BRIEN

The memory, fading now with age and a little confused, recalls a slip of a girl who spent the whole Saturday in the shop. Just out of school, the girl examined the bookshelves with an intensity unusual in one so young. When, at the end of the day, in the polite conversation that ensued as the girl made her purchase, Mother asked her what she hoped to be, Edna O'Brien's answer was clear and confident, 'I am training to be a writer.'

In twentieth-century Ireland, few learnt the craft better but none were to suffer more because of it. Always totally honest to herself and her art (her continuous question is: 'is it writing?'), Enda O'Brien has never compromised the truth as she perceives it and she has become very much the conscience of modern Ireland. Because of her candid approach, she has brought upon her head not only the opprobrium of Church and state but the suspicion and mistrust of her peers. Despite her undoubted position as one of Ireland's leading writers, Edna O'Brien has never enjoyed a popular press in Ireland and to a large extent her literary achievement as a writer and commentator has never been fully understood or properly evaluated.

She was born in the County Clare village of Tuamgraney in 1930 and educated in Loughrea, County Galway, and Dublin. In 1957, she left Dublin and settled in London where she still lives. Although her marriage with Ernest Gebler produced two sons, it was an unhappy one and they divorced in 1967.

The publication of *The Country Girls* in 1960 not only announced a major new Irish writer but also signalled the birth of a whole new indigenous literary movement, the first in the independent state to address domestic and religious issues with candour and to question the religious and social status quo in a way that was almost taboo. That a young woman should dare do this was to demonstrate a remarkable personal courage.

From the first sentence, the prose is deceptively simple:

> I wakened quickly and sat up in bed abruptly. It is only when I am anxious that I waken easily and for a minute I did not know why my heart was beating faster than usual. Then I remembered. The old reason. He had not come home.

Immediately the reader is drawn into the life of the young teenage girl, Kate Brady, who lives in fear of the periodic drunken bouts of a spendthrift and volatile father whose reckless profligacy almost leads to the loss of the farm. Kate is sent to a convent boarding school. Kate's friend Baba conspires to get them expelled and they head for the bright city lights of Dublin. Never mind that they are in a poorish boarding house and Kate is working as a grocer's assistant: their hunger for life is unquenchable and so our contrasting heroines burst their way into it.

The simplicity of the tale belies the extraordinary skill with which Edna O'Brien presents the full panorama of life in the rural Ireland of the 1950s, its hypocrisies and suffocating intellectual climate. O'Brien underlines the difficulties young women of independent mind encountered at that time in achieving their potential. With all this, the novel is not without its moments of laconic humour and unexpected kindnesses. The slip of a girl learned her craft well.

The Great O'Neill

SEAN O'FAOLAIN

Sean O'Faolain was probably the best full-back of the twentieth-century Irish book world. Born in Cork at the beginning of the century and living until 1991, he was the quintessential man of letters. Outside his varied career as a writer, his most lasting contribution to Irish culture was as the co-founder of *The Bell* magazine which he edited from its first issue in October 1940 until 1946. The aim of the magazine was to introduce international literature into an increasingly isolationist country and to combat the narrow-minded censorship current in Ireland at the time. It also provided a platform for social, cultural and political debate on Irish issues as well as giving Irish writers their most significant shop window to reach an audience since the founding of the state.

O'Faolain was educated by the Presentation Brothers in Cork and then went to UCC, where he was greatly inspired by the writer Daniel Corkery. The executions of the 1916 leaders had a traumatic effect on him. He became involved with the Gaelic League and the republican movement but was quickly disillusioned when he realised that neither movement had the necessary skills to realise their political or social aspirations. He took an MA in English literature at Harvard University and taught in Strawberry Hill, London, before, on the advice of Edward Garnett, the publisher's reader at Jonathan Cape, he returned to Ireland in 1933 to become a writer.

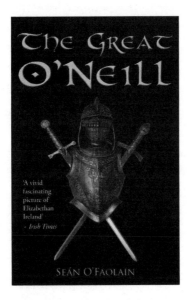

THE GREAT
O'NEILL

'A vivid
fascinating
picture of
Elizabethan
Ireland'
- *Irish Times*

SEÁN O'FAOLAIN

O'Faolain's fame is based mainly on his short stories, but he also wrote novels, books of criticism, travel, social commentary and biographies, the most significant of which are *The King of the Beggars* and *The Great O'Neill*, published in 1942. The latter remains the most comprehensive life yet published of Hugh O'Neill, Earl of Tyrone, who rebelled against the Tudor colonization of Ireland and whose defeat at Kinsale in 1601 signalled the demise of Gaelic Ireland.

By using two relatively minor events in early-16th-century Ireland, O'Faolain builds the political and social panorama that existed at the time and places the figure of the young O'Neill at the juncture of two cultures. Along with this he documents O'Neill's education in an English home, thus explaining the dilemmas which faced him when he returned to Ireland in 1568.

Along with this carefully-created picture, O'Faolain takes a little jump backwards to bring us through the Desmond Rebellion and the effect it had on the young O'Neill.

Out of this picture O'Neill the man, soldier and politician emerges. Once he declares his Irish allegiance, the rebellion develops at an increasing speed until it reaches its final débâcle and the book ends with O'Neill's final sad days of exile in Rome.

Throughout the narration, the author skilfully keeps us aware of the European dimension of the rebellion – O'Neill may have been the first Irish statesman to have impacted on international politics – and the defeat at Kinsale, we discover, had a much greater impact on the Counter-Reformation than had been acknowledged.

We can imagine that when O'Faolain finished the last page of the book he calmly filled his pipe with tobacco and had a long and intellectually satisfying smoke.

The Collected Stories

LIAM O'FLAHERTY

There is often a machine-gun rhythm in the writing of Liam O'Flaherty: words are spat out in quick succession and with a tremendous energy. This is particularly the case when his subject is a peasant struggling against nature or raw human instincts. However, when the theme is the natural world, the tone tends to soften and the rhythm of the prose becomes gentle, almost tender. No matter what the mood is, it is always immediate and subject to sudden change. This invests the stories with an excitement rarely achieved in the genre and is one of the reasons why Liam O'Flaherty has strong claims to be among the finest short-story writers in any literature.

O'Flaherty was born the ninth of ten children on Inis Mór, the largest of the Aran Islands, in 1896. His father was a Land Leaguer while his mother was descended from a Plymouth Brethren family that had come from County Antrim to build lighthouses on the islands. He was educated locally and at Rockwell College, County Tipperary where he became a postulant to the Holy Ghost Fathers. He abandoned this in 1915 and, using his mothers' name of Ganly, joined the Irish Guards.

He was wounded during a bombardment at Langmark in September 1917. This was to result in an acute melancholia which was to affect him for the rest of his life and may explain the sudden mood swings that affect his writing. After indulging in radical politics for a period, he became a restless wanderer,

travelling the world before returning to Dublin, where he finally settled down. In his later years he became more and more reclusive. He died in 1984.

He was the author of a number of novels and some volumes of autobiography, but it is in the short-story form that O'Flaherty's true strength lies. He published several collections, including one in Irish entitled *Dúil*. In 1999 all the stories were collected and edited by A.A. Kelly and published by Seamus Cashman of the Wolfhound Press in a superbly handsome three-volume set with slipcase.

Although the writing of these stories spanned more than fifty years, they never lose their immediacy. Also, there is no knowing where the next story is going to lead, going from an in-depth description of a wave from its genesis to its apotheosis in crashing against a cliff, to the convalescent yard of a workhouse hospital where a visiting tramp berates two more prominent inmates for their lack of initiative.

O'Flaherty has an amazing ability to bring you straight into the heart of his stories, most of which begin with a quick short sentence that is totally absolute. 'The idea came in a flash,' or 'Brunton was waiting in the select bar,' or 'He was eight feet long.' The reader simply can't wait to get to the next sentence. Yet, O'Flaherty retains control, bringing the reader delightfully to the conclusion.

All the time one senses that O'Flaherty is laughing and his enjoyment is infectious. Even when the human species is seen at its most tragic or desperate there is always present a celebration of life.

The Lonely Passion of Judith Hearne

BRIAN MOORE

International business travel has its own frustrations – and opportunities. Finding myself unexpectedly stuck in Toronto of a Saturday, I decided to follow an old tactic of Father's known as 'paying for the petrol'. To this end, I sought out and found some antiquarian bookshops in the hope of discovering a few gems at reasonable prices whose resale value would help to alleviate the considerable expense of the trip.

The first three shops proved to be fruitless and the fourth wasn't much better until, a little dispirited, I was led by curiosity to the Canadian literature section. To my surprise and delight, more than half the section consisted of Brian Moore first editions, including the four extremely rare potboiler crime novels which he had published anonymously or under a pseudonym while learning his craft and which he had refused to recognise as his own work in later life.

In better spirits, I couldn't resist chiding the bookseller for trying to claim the son of Ulster, Brian Moore, as a Canadian writer.

'Give me a break,' he replied sheepishly. 'You guys have enough. Allow us to claim at least one decent writer.'

The bookseller had a point. Although born in Belfast in 1921, where he spent the first twenty-seven years of his life, Moore emigrated to Canada and took citizenship there in 1953. It was while working in the *Montreal Gazette* that he wrote his first three

novels. He moved to the US in 1959, ending up in California, where he died in 1999. He never relinquished his Canadian passport.

Moore was to write seventeen novels as well as short stories and film scripts. His great classic, as he himself would have it, is his first novel *Judith Hearne*, published in 1955 and republished in 1956 as *The Lonely Passion of Judith Hearne*.

The diminutive, pathetic figure of Judith Hearne remains a colossus in the pantheon of modern Irish literature. The reader first meets her as she moves into yet another seedy furnished room and watches her attempt to make a home out of her drab surroundings. Alone, a spinster, she is the epitome of genteel respectability, building her self-esteem on false premises and well-worn clichés.

From these foundations, Moore takes the reader deeper and deeper into the soul of this lonely woman, setting her amongst a cast of equally desperate and impoverished characters in a world where every penny spent is a matter of concern and whose byword is failure. Her one solace is her Sunday-afternoon visit to the comfortable middle-class O'Neill family but even here she is a figure of fun and derision.

Into this sad environment rides an unlikely knight in shining armour, the returned Yank, Madden, who is also building castles in the air. For Hearne, he becomes her last chance, while he sees in her a potential investor in a dubious business venture. It is his rejection of her that causes Hearne's final breakdown.

Written with empathy and sensitivity, *The Lonely Passion of Judith Hearne* is a monument to the countless women who were imprisoned by a society and a religion indifferent to their individual humanity: condemned to lives of loneliness and silent desperation.

Tales From Bective Bridge

Mary Lavin

The abiding memory is of a rather statuesque woman, arms folded over chest, shoulders firmly back, holding court in the middle of the shop speaking with tremendous volubility, without pause. It didn't matter whether the audience was two, two hundred, or two thousand, she told story after story in an unceasing flow of celebration and magic. The real wonder was that Mary Lavin ever drew breath long enough to write the stories she did in such an even and apparently simple style, leaving us the rich legacy of so many fine volumes of these treasures, more especially her first wonderful collection *Tales from Bective Bridge*.

Born of Irish parents in Massachusetts in 1912, Mary Lavin moved to Ireland when she was ten years of age. She lived for some time in her mother's home in Athenry, County Galway, and was educated at the Loreto College on St Stephen's Green, Dublin and at UCD, where she completed an MA thesis on Jane Austen. The remainder of her life was spent between Bective, County Meath and Dublin. She died in 1996.

Lavin's style is disarmingly simple. Her approach is direct and to the point. When asked once why she encircled her name every time she signed a book, her reply was: 'Because that's the way I sign my name.' It was possibly this directness that attracted Lord Dunsany to her writing. He was so taken by her mastery that he was instrumental in the publication of her first collection, *Tales from Bective Bridge*, in 1943 and wrote the preface for it.

Lavin's versatility as a writer and command of the genre is evident in each of the stories in the collection. There is always present a sensitive and ironic observation of human nature which gives the stories a wry humour and this adds immeasurably to the enjoyment of reading them.

This wry humour is at its best in 'Brother Boniface.' Although considered by his parents to be slow and something of a failure, Barney finds solace in the life of the monastery where his apparent failures are neatly accommodated and he finally hears 'the bells of silence.' In 'Miss Holland', the humour is more savage when the timid Miss Holland's sad attempt at sociability is crudely smashed by her more vulgar fellow-lodgers.

With this somewhat laconic view of the human condition, Lavin also instils into the stories a real sense of the tragic side of life. In 'The Green Grave and the Black Grave', the cultural differences between the people on the mainland and the people on the islands are bemusedly scrutinised and a deeply ironic conclusion reached while the tragic intensity of the old woman's mourning for her son in 'The Dead Soldier' has strong parallels with Maurya's mourning in Synge's *Riders to the Sea*.

The stories in *Tales from Bective Bridge* are written in a delightfully refreshing style. They are so full of surprises that the reader is as constantly enthralled by the content as by the artistry of the writing. This extraordinary collection of short stories has all the hallmarks of a masterpiece.

An tOileánach

Tomás Ó Croimhthain

Má cheapann tú go raibh saol álainn rómánsúil ag na daoine a raibh cónaí orthu ar an mBlascaod Mór i dtús an fichiú haois, léireoidh na chéad leathanaigh den leabhar *An tOileánach* nach amhlaidh a bhí. Bhí saol crua, deacair ag na hoileánaigh ó bhreith go bás. Bhíodh coimhlintí síoraí idir iad féin agus an nádúr, an t-ocras agus an galar agus is minic a d'fhulaing siad bás tobann ina dteaghlaigh féin.

Ag tosú i 1929 leis an leabhar *An tOileánach*, foilsíodh na trí leabhar ar a bhfuil 'Litríocht na nOileán' bunaithe. As sin amach, usáideadh na téacsanna sin chun seansaol na nGael a mholadh mar shaghas Útóipe agus múineadh an litríocht seo i scoileanna na tíre ar shlí is go raibh drochmheas ag formhór na tíre ar na hoileánaigh agus ar a slí beatha. Nuair a léitear, afách, an chéad leabhar den tsraith sin, gan reamhthuiscint ar bith, feictear gur leabhar den scoth é agus, cosúil le gach leabhar eile den ardchaighdeán céanna, is fiú é a léamh i dteanga ar bith. Níl aon amhras ach go bhfuil cur síos macanta ar staid an chine dhaonna sa leabhar *An tOileánach*.

Rugadh Tomás Ó Criomhthain ar an mBlascaod Mór in 1855. Tar éis saol fada a bhí crua go leor – an cineál saoil a ndéantar cur síos air ina shárshaothar – chuir sé suim ina theanga dhúchais. Mhúin sé Gaeilge don dream a thug cuairt ar an oileán sna fichidí, leithéidí Carl Marstrander, Alfred O'Rahilly agus Brian Ó Ceallaigh. Ba é an Ceallach a spreag é chun dialann

a choinneáil. Foilsíodh an dialann i 1928 faoin teideal *Allagar na hInse*. Foilsíodh a bheathaisnéis i 1929 faoin teideal *An tOileánach*. Bhí an saothar seo ina bhunchloch do genre nua i litríocht na Gaeilge, 'Beathaisnéis na Gaeltachta'. Cailleadh an Criomhthanach i 1937.

In 1937, Robin Flower, the Oxford don who had become a frequent visitor to the Blaskets (and the first to document life on the Island in his book *The Western Island*) published *The Islandman*, the English translation of *An tOileánach*. Since then Flower's translation has seldom, if ever, been out of print. Its popularity is due, in part, to the book's status as the first of its genre but, more importantly it is due to the strong individual style of O'Crohan (the English version of Ó Criomhthain) whose sole purpose in writing *The Islandman* was to 'set down the character of the people about me so that some record of us might live after us, for the like of us will never be again.'

Basic, natural, raw, tragic, humorous, laconic, ironic, self-effacing, resilient, observant and, above all, human – all these attributes are evident in this extraordinarily lively narration. Ó Criomhthain celebrates life to the fullest and, while not being overtly religious, gives witness to a deep spirituality that enables him to handle with resignation the almost casual tragedies endemic to island life.

An tOileánach/The Islandman is one of the world's great indigenous classics.

Give Them Stones

MARY BECKETT

To many people interested in Irish lore and literature, the name Mary Beckett would probably suggest a female relative of Ireland's third Nobel Laureate. This is not surprising as the literary output of the person now in question is modest, being confined to one collection of short stories, some children's books and two novels. Biographical detail is also scarce. Mary Beckett was born in Belfast in 1926 into a family of teachers. She herself became a teacher and taught in the Ardoyne area of her native city until her marriage in 1956, after which she moved to Dublin, where she still lives.

In her twenties she began writing short stories but she stopped writing while she raised her two daughters and three sons. Her stories were collected by David Marcus and published in 1980 by that unsung hero of modern Irish publishing, Philip MacDermott, with the title *A Belfast Woman*. The novel *Give Them Stones* was published in 1987.

Give Them Stones relates the story of Martha Murtagh, a working-class girl who grew up in Belfast before the Second World War. As was the norm, her mother was the wage-earner while her father found it impossible to find work. From the opening sentence, the pace of the first-person narrative is so even, the language so intimate and straightforward, that for a lot of the time the book reads like an autobiography. Only gradually does it emerge that it is, in fact, a work of fiction.

The Second World War breaks out and Belfast is blitzed. For safety reasons the children are evacuated to the country. Although her siblings return quickly to Belfast, Martha remains with her aged aunts for the course of the war. Here, she matures into an independent young woman developing an interest in reading and baking. By the time the family is reunited Martha has inherited her aunts' tiny holding.

The narrative then takes on a new rhythm as Martha's life unfolds for the next twenty years. She leaves school to work in a mill, her sister becomes a teacher and marries, while her feckless brother becomes involved in Republican circles. Her father has been unjustly interred and dies a bitter man. Martha takes an interest in the Irish language and enrols in a night course to learn it. Here she meets Dermot and knows she is going to marry him when she sees his gas stove.

Subsequently, in Martha's indifferent marriage, it is the same gas stove that allows her some small financial independence. While she raises her four sons she bakes bread and scones and sells them to neighbours. Through her the reader watches the beginnings of the Civil Rights Movement, the Falls Road curfew of the 1970s, the bombings, the burnings, internment. Martha fears for her four jobless sons: no street is safe for them to walk on without the British Army 'lifting' them or the Provos attempting to recruit them.

A simple-enough story perhaps, but this book is so much more – it is a monument to the struggles and courage of an ordinary working mother who attempts to carve out a decent life for herself and her family in the midst if civil turmoil and violence.

The Great Hunger

CECIL WOODHAM SMITH

First published in 1962, and having since survived two generations without once going out of print, *The Great Hunger, Ireland 1845-1849* remains the best single volume relating the story of Ireland's most devastating and sustained national disaster, the Great Famine. The result of at least ten years' research, it is almost a step-by-step narrative of the dreadful events that occurred in Ireland from the first intimations of the potato blight appearing in Ireland in 1845 until Queen Victoria's visit to the country in the summer of 1849.

Cecil Blanche Woodham-Smith was born in Wales on 29 April 1896. Her father, Colonel James Fitzgerald, had served in the Indian Army during the Sepoy Mutiny, while her mother's family included General Sir Thomas Picton, who was killed at Waterloo. Cecil Woodham-Smith graduated from Oxford in 1917 with a second-class degree in English. In 1928, she married George Ivan Woodham-Smith, with whom she had an exceptionally deep relationship until his death in 1968. Before her two children went to boarding school she wrote potboilers which were useful in improving her undoubted narrative skills. Her real strength, however, was in historical writing and it was in this genre that she first made her mark when her biography of Florence Nightingale was published in 1950. Three years later *The Reason Why*, her account of the 'Charge of the Light Brigade' during the Crimean War, appeared. She published the first volume of *Queen Victoria:*

Her Life and Times in 1972. She died at the age of eighty in 1977 before she could complete the second volume.

Woodham-Smith's approach is direct, straightforward and strictly chronological. She excels in bringing her reader on board with her as though she has just met a long-lost friend and has some fascinating news to tell. This gift becomes apparent from the first chapter of *The Great Hunger* as she gives the historical background to her story. She then describes the contemporary political situation in England, the rural conditions in Ireland, and reminds us that Ireland had suffered many partial famines in the thirty years prior to 1845.

Hardly pausing, she takes us to the events of 1845, moving deftly from the failure of the potato crop in Ireland to the political response (or lack of it) in England. Here her narrative powers really blossom and her enthusiasm for the subject rubs off on the reader. Given the depressing nature of the subject-matter, this is a remarkable achievement.

Another striking element of the book is its structure. As she moves through the narration the author keeps the reader informed of all the multifarious elements of the famine – the nature of the potato blight, the different strains of the fevers that became epidemic, the various means of emigration, the nuts and bolts of the tortuous attempts the British administration made to deal with the crisis, the pathetic political response of Irish nationalists – without once losing sight of her main story. It is a masterly achievement.

Booking Passage

Thomas Lynch

A book launch on a hot summer's evening. As the invited guests begin to gather, the author takes me out the gallery door on to Middle Street where he presents me with a small package. I open it and discover a ring in the shape of a coffin.

'That's like the Claddagh ring,' he said. 'When the crown is pointing towards the heart it means the wearer is bespoke, when pointing towards the nail, still available. A coffin will always go into the church head first. If you wear this ring with the head pointing outwards, you're as healthy as a bird; pointing towards the heart, you're goose is cooked.' The episode was a prime example of the macabre humour of Thomas Lynch, American, Irishman, undertaker, poet and essayist. The occasion was the launch of his first book of essays, *The Undertaking*, in 1997.

Eight years later *Booking Passage* is published. Subtitled 'We Irish and Americans', it defies classification, being at once memoir, meditation, travelogue, philosophical/literary treatise and cultural study. But above all it is a guidebook, as Lynch himself calls it, for those 'fellow pilgrims' seeking out their own cultural, personal and larger human identities:

> I've measured such moments against that first night
> in Moveen where staring into the firmament, pissing
> among the whitethorn trees, I had the first inkling that
> I was at once one and only and one of a kind, apart

from my people yet among them still, the same as every other human being, but different, my own history afloat on all history, my name and the names of my kinsmen repeating themselves down generations, time bearing us all effortlessly, like the sea with its moon-driven, undulant possibilities: we Irish, we Americans, the faithfully departed, the stargazers at the sea's edge of every island of every hemisphere of every planet, all of us the same but different.

Essentially the book tells the story of the Lynch family, most of whom were forced to emigrate from famine-stricken Ireland. They finally set up in Milford, Michigan, as undertakers. Throughout the generations, some family link is kept with the west Clare holding and the book opens with the jet-lagged author, the first to return, walking up the laneway and meeting his two cousins, twice removed and unmarried, who have managed to survive on the old farm. Using his own family history as a platform, Lynch meditates on the ethnic variations of human beings, their beliefs, aspirations and racial fanaticisms. We watch Lynch establish himself as a published poet, inherit his cousins' cottage and develop a writer's retreat there while never losing touch with his calling as undertaker.

Every so often his mordant sense of humour surfaces, as when he relates his experience at a Clare wake where he overhears the widow informing her parish priest that her husband died from gonorrhoea. The blushing churchman dealt with this as diplomatically as possible but the daughter began to scold her mother, saying that her father hadn't died from gonorrhoea but 'dirrhea'.

'Hush my lovely,' the woman said, holding her daughter's face in her hands. 'I'd rather your father be remembered for the great lover he never was than the big shit he always seemed to be.'

From Bantry Bay to Leitrim

Peter Somerville-Large

In every national history there appears to be an event which was of no real significance in terms of its political or social development, yet stands out as a singular achievement and, for some reason, is seen to define the ethos of the nation. The event warrants little more than a paragraph in the general histories of the country and may be the subject of the occasional political ballad but it will always be a romantic symbol of nationalist bravery and courage. Such an event was the ill-fated O'Sullivan Beare retreat from west Cork after the battle of Kinsale to the safety of County Leitrim and refuge with Brian Óg O'Rourke.

In the foreword to *From Bantry Bay to Leitrim*, published in 1974, Peter Somerville-Large writes:

> It was suggested to me that one way of getting a clearer understanding of the extent of O'Sullivan's achievement was by following the route that he and his followers took. The more I thought about this idea the more interested I became in carrying it out. I planned to walk it in midwinter, setting out on the last day of the year, stopping at the places he did, seeking out traditions about his flight. This I managed to do during January 1972.

From the moment his wife drops him off at a bridge outside Bantry to the moment four weeks later when a woman points to a

sign over his head that says 'Leitrim one mile', Somerville-Large enthrals us not just with the narrative of the retreat but with his own experiences as he retraces O'Sullivan Beare's footsteps.

Born in 1928 in Dublin, Peter Somerville-Large had a comfortable upbringing. After graduating from Trinity College, he was variously a lecturer in the Royal Military Academy, Kabul, Afganistan, a gold miner in Australia and a journalist. He has written several books relating to Ireland as well as travel books on the Yemen and Iran.

After a fifty-page introduction in which the author describes in some detail the historical background to the journey, we set off with him, as he follows the path taken by the O'Sullivan Beare as closely as he can. There follows a marvellous mixture of ancient and contemporary lore, relating not just to the retreat itself but to other aspects of local history encountered along the way.

There is the exotic tale of Maria Dolores Eliza Rosanna Gilbert, born at Castle Oliver in County Limerick in 1818, who became notorious throughout Europe as Lola Montez and whose exploits included 'throwing her garters and drawers at a Parisian audience, horse-whipping a Berlin policeman, causing a riot in Poland and dancing on the tables during a civic reception in Bonn at a time when Queen Victoria was paying a state visit.'

The book is full of such gems but Somerville-Large never loses sight of the main journey. The reader feels comfortable in his company and doesn't want to leave it. There is a strong element of drawing the armchairs around the fire about this book.

Bailegangáire

Thomas Murphy

There is a story told that, during a spell in hospital, the actress Siobhán McKenna was visited by the playwright Tom Murphy, who told her that she needed to recover quickly as he had written a play specifically for her. The story may or may not be true but while it is certain that Murphy was the writer of *Bailegangáire* (published by the Gallery Press in 1986), it is also indisputable that when the play was first produced by Druid Theatre in Galway on the 5 December 1985, McKenna made the character of Mommo her own.

Born in 1935, Murphy grew up the youngest of ten children in Tuam, County Galway, where he attended the local Christian Brothers and technical schools. After winning a scholarship he became a metalwork teacher in Mountbellew, near Tuam. He began writing plays towards the end of the 1950s. He had two plays rejected by the Abbey Theatre before going to London in 1961 to work full-time as a writer. After several successful plays written during the 1960s, the most significant being *Famine* in 1968, Murphy moved back to Dublin in 1970. From 1983 to 1985, he was writer-in-association with Druid Theatre in Galway, during which time he produced a totally revamped version of an earlier play *The White House* under the title *Conversations on a Homecoming* as well as that masterpiece of the modern Irish theatre: *Bailegangáire*.

Although born in Belfast, Siobhán McKenna grew up in

Galway. She began her acting career in Taibhdhearc na Gaillimhe in 1944 and later acquired a significant international reputation as an actor on stage and screen. She was particularly famous for her various roles depicting strong women, such as Pegeen Mike in *The Playboy of the Western World*, Saint Joan in the Bernard Shaw play of that name and Cass Maguire in Brian Friel's *The Loves of Cass Maguire*. It is not altogether surprising that Tom Murphy should create the character of Mommo for her in *Bailegangáire*. Her inspirational and unrivalled interpretation of this role was to be her swan song, as she died within a year of the inaugural performance.

At first glance *Bailegangáire* is about three women: Mommo, who is senile, and her two granddaughters: Mary, her minder, and Dolly who is pregnant but doesn't know who the father is.

Once Murphy has set down the basic lines of the symphony it begins to gather pace with Mommo as the central character. In her apparently senseless rambling she repeats the never-ending tale of how Bailegangáire received its name, encouraged by Mary to finish the tale so that she can pick up the threads of normal living again. Enter Dolly, who brings an element of harsh reality into the story but who is also trying to escape an increasing desperation.

The pace increases, Mommo's tale gathers momentum, her words pouring out in an unending torrent hastening towards an elusive climax with Mary pushing towards a final resolution and Dolly seeking a pragmatic escape. The play is not without a sense of hope as the three women find a degree of consolation in their communal suffering.

The Journey Home

Dermot Bolger

It is difficult to conceive that barely thirty years ago Ireland was on the verge of fiscal and moral bankruptcy. The promises of the 1960s had failed to materialise, the political, judicial and religious mentors of the country were showing alarming signs of corruption and the optimistic idealism of the civil rights movement in Northern Ireland had deteriorated into a morass of violence. The dole queues were lengthening and the safety-valve of emigration was cut off. To the coming-of-age generation, Ireland was a country with an irrelevant past, a depressing present and a shaky future.

As is normal in such an environment, the raised voices of youth were in the main stifled and would have remained so were it not for a small number of courageous publishers who struggled to give these voices a platform from which to vent their protest and anger. One such publisher was Dermot Bolger, who founded Raven Arts Press in 1977.

Born in Finglas in 1959, Bolger grew up in a working-class environment which later formed the basis of most of his work. Educated at St Canice's and Beneavin College, he worked as a factory hand and a library assistant before committing himself completely to writing and publishing. Poet, novelist and playwright as well as publisher, Bolger has proven himself to be champion of the voice of protest and his novel, *The Journey Home*, first published in 1990, is his own singular and powerful

contribution to that voice.

The Journey Home tells the story of Francis Hanrahan (Hano) who has been raised on the northern outskirts of Dublin in a new estate that is neither rural nor urban. As his father loses his grip on his own cultural identity, Hano becomes more and more rootless. His parents' dependence on local magnates, the Plunketts, further erodes his sense of identity.

He receives an offer of temporary employment in the Voters' Registry Office where he meets Shay, who introduces him to Dublin's subculture and nightlife. For the first time Hano experiences freedom and a sense of belonging, but Shay, despite his brash confidence, also proves to be vulnerable and becomes a victim of the harsh cultural politics of the time. His downfall and final humiliation triggers in Hano a catharsis which he shares with the enigmatic Kate and together they come to a sense of their real home, a sense that is loosely defined by Hano himself: 'Home was not the place where you were born but the place you created for yourself, where you finally became what you were.'

Despite the sense of futility and anger that constantly informs the narration, *The Journey Home* is not without its sense of hope. The book is imbued with sudden flashes of humour and surprising moments of generosity. The hypocrisies of Irish life are fully and uncompromisingly presented but so are its strengths and inherent decencies.

An Duanaire 1600-1900: Poems of the Dispossessed

SEÁN Ó TUAMA AND THOMAS KINSELLA

Déantar dearmad minic go leor gurbh í an Ghaeilge an teanga ba mhó a bhí á labhairt in Éirinn go dtí aimsir an Ghorta Mhóir, cé go raibh sí á labhairt in áiteanna éagsúla ar fud na tíre i bhfad ina dhiaidh sin freisin. Dá bhrí sin, is féidir a rá gurbh í litríocht na Gaeilge litríocht na hÉireann suas go dtí deireadh an naoú haois déag. Tá an-saibhreas sa litríocht sin, go háirithe sa bhfilíocht. Bhí an baol ann, áfach, go gcaillfeadh gnáthphobal na hÉireann an fhilíocht seo go léir go dtí gur fhoilsigh Preas Dolmen *An Duanaire 1600-1900: Poems of the Dispossessed* in 1981.

The Dolmen Press was founded by Liam Miller, an architect, and his wife Josephine in 1951, and for the next thirty-six years it was the shining star of the Irish publishing industry. From a shaky start it grew to have an international reputation for the quality of its book design. It also broke new ground by championing emerging Irish poets such as John Montague and Thomas Kinsella. Its most famous publications are the magnificent version of the ancient Irish epic *The Táin Bó Cuailgne* (1969) translated by Kinsella with brush drawings by Louis Le Brocquy, and *An Duanaire*, the bilingual anthology of Irish poetry written between 1600 and 1900, edited by Seán Ó Tuama and with verse translations by Kinsella, published in 1981.

Corkman Seán Ó Tuama was an Irish scholar and academic. Born in 1926, he published several classic studies of the major Irish-language poets, edited a number of poetry anthologies and

produced some volumes of his own poetry.

Thomas Kinsella, born in Dublin in 1928, established himself as a major Irish poet, publishing his first collections in the early 1950s and immersing himself in intensive studies of Old and Middle Irish language and literature, which culminated in his magnificent translation of *The Táin Bó Cuailgne* and the partnership with Ó Tuama and Miller which produced *An Duanaire*.

In the deceptively simple introduction to *An Duanaire* the reader is first given the background to Irish literary culture, then taken through the various forms of poetic expression such as the aisling, occasional verse and pre-Renaissance modes. The authors claim: 'The primary aim of this anthology is to demonstrate the nature and quality of a part of the Irish poetic tradition to readers with some knowledge of modern Irish,' and: 'Daoine a bhfuil Nua-Ghaeilge éigin acu is mó a bhainfidh leas, dar linn, as an duanaire seo.'

In fact it is a modest claim. This anthology affords the reader who has no Irish at all a rare opportunity to enjoy the full depth and richness of its poetry. The work is presented in such a way that the reader can fully understand the sentiments and the context of each individual poem, while appreciating the wide range of its rhythms and the extraordinary sensitivities of its language.

Traits and Stories of the Irish Peasantry

WILLIAM CARLETON

Calmness personified, his eyes slowly wandered over the mound of Liscannor stone that had arrived on our front garden. Then, assured and unhurried, he proceeded to metamorphosise the hole in our sitting room into the cheerful fireplace that is now the centre of our home. Like a conductor of a symphony orchestra, every gesture had a meaning so that within three hours, the fireplace looked as if it had been there forever.

With the job completed to his satisfaction, he sat at our dining room table with a cup of tea perusing the books on the shelves and asked: 'Have ye ever heard of the man Willie Carleton? Now, there was a real craftsman.'

Coming from a stone mason, master craftsman and thorough gentleman some one hundred and sixty years after William Carleton had penned his *Traits and Stories*, this praise from Michael Clerkin was surely among the highest accolades that Carleton could ever hope to have.

Born in County Tyrone in 1794, the youngest of fourteen children in a family of Irish-speaking farmers, William Carleton was to survive Irish peasant life, membership of a secret agrarian society, eviction, the tribulations of the itinerant teacher and near destruction in 1820s Dublin to carve a niche for himself in the Irish literary pantheon.

He was to become the first writer from an Irish-speaking peasant background to describe in English the realities of Irish

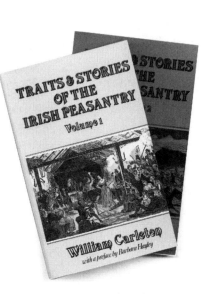

TRAITS & STORIES
OF THE
IRISH PEASANTRY
Volume 1

William Carleton

with a preface by Barbara Hayley

rural life. He produced many novels and short stories and was in the throes of writing his autobiography when he died in 1869. He was Ireland's first seriously popular writer and while his novel *Willie Reilly and his Dear Colleen Bawn* published in 1855 could claim to be his bestseller, his reputation was based on his *Traits and Stories of Irish Peasantry*, the first series of which was published in 1830.

In one of the stories 'Geography of an Irish Oath', Carleton begins with the comments:

> No pen can do justice to the extravagance and frolic inseparable from the character of the Irish people; nor has any system of philosophy been discovered that can with moral fitness be applied to them.

From the moment we meet Ned McKeown, we are, as it were, thrown in at the deep end. We go to Shane Faed's wedding and Larry McFarland's wake. We witness the station, the battle of the factions. We follow in the footsteps of the Lough Derg pilgrim and attend the hedge school. We go to midnight Mass and hear of the horse stealers and Phil Purcell the pig-driver. We wonder at the Lianhan shee, prepare to enter the seminary at Maynooth and empathise with the poor scholar. We are told of the dark deeds that are perpetrated at the Wildgoose Lodge and the Red Well.

Not once in all of this does the pace slacken. Carleton was the first to explore the depths of what has become known as Hiberno-English and he does this with tremendous energy.

Fools of Fortune

WILLIAM TREVOR

William Trevor is one of Irish literature's enigmas. He wafts like a ghost across the literary landscape and when he chooses to make his presence felt, he does so with devastating effect. Then he withdraws into the shadows again, and again, when least expected, produces yet another incredible novel or collection of short stories imbued with deep insights and a warm understanding of human frailties. His protagonists are generally ordinary people living ordinary lives, but whose lives are governed by fatal quirks of character or whose fate is determined by social conditions beyond their control. Nowhere is this more evident than in his sophisticated novel of the War of Independence, *Fools of Fortune*, first published in 1983.

William Trevor was born William Cox in Mitchelstown, County Cork in 1928, the son of a Protestant bank official. He was to have a nomadic upbringing as his father was transferred to a number of rural branches before settling in Dublin.

After graduating from Trinity College, Trevor taught for a while in Ireland before emigrating to England, where for a period he became a moderately successful sculptor. Eventually, though, he became a writer: his first novel, *A Standard of Behaviour*, was published in 1958. Since then, he has been extraordinarily prolific, producing novel after novel as well as several collections of short stories. Some of the stories have been successfully adapted as television films, the most famous being *The Ballroom of Romance*,

the title story of a collection published in 1972.

In *Fools of Fortune*, Trevor makes clever use of the Big House as a fulcrum to explore how the War of Independence affected three major cultures: the English, the Anglo-Irish and the Irish. By uniting the Woodcombe family of Woodcombe Park in Dorset, England with the Quintan family of the big house of Kilneagh near Fermoy, County Cork through a series of coincidental marriages down the generations, he creates a wonderful platform to examine the full effects of the Troubles on the descendants of the two houses as well as the local inhabitants of the Cork village.

Having set this up, he adds an informer, a lynching and a horrific reprisal, all mixed in with stories of requited and unrequited love, dreadful and fatal grief, unadulterated vengeance and insanity. The prose is so gentle, it's as if Trevor is taking the reader by the hand through all this mayhem with calmness, detachment and occasional touches of humour. Then, without warning, and in that wonderful incisive way of his, he stings with a sharp sentence or two that heightens the tension and underlines the real tragedy of violent conflict.

Trevor has an amazing capacity to surprise the reader and one of the more fascinating features of *Fools of Fortune* is its range of intriguing characters. This gives the novel tremendous depth. Although the landscape of the book is wide and varied, Trevor never loses control of the narrative. His prose is so masterly that the storyteller disappears behind the story.

Ireland's Civil War

CALTON YOUNGER

The period from 1916 to 1923, known euphemistically as 'The Troubles', has resulted in more books than any other momentous event in Irish history. The flow of general histories, personal memories, local accounts, historic and political analyses of social and economic effects, novels, plays, poems, songs and folklore has been unceasing. In fact, over the last few years, it has been increasing as the centenary of the 1916 Rising hovers on the horizon. With all that, however, it is difficult to identify one single volume that gives a relatively balanced chronological and straightforward account of that tumultuous period. Calton Younger's *Ireland's Civil War*, first published in 1968, has strong claims to do just that.

'When I was a small boy,' Younger tells us, 'I read a story about Ireland's Civil War in an annual. The heroes, young Republican soldiers in the mountains, had to fight for their lives against an overwhelming force of villainous "Staters". My sympathies were strongly engaged and still lingered when I began to write this book.'

In 1966, after the fiftieth anniversary of the Rising, there was a rush of publications in Dublin and elsewhere relating to the events of Easter Week 1916, all of them strongly influenced by the then prevailing philosophy that the blood sacrifice suffered by the rebels was pure and necessary so that Ireland could rise phoenix-like out of the putrid ashes of English rule. The majority

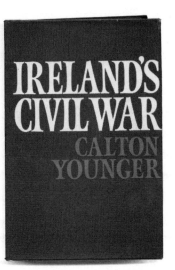

IRELAND'S
CIVIL WAR

CALTON
YOUNGER

of these books were written by survivors of the rebellion, their families and associates and, understandably, conveyed a strong sense of pride tinged with triumphalism.

In this context, the pragmatic approach of Englishman Calton Younger was like a breath of fresh air. The fact that a book on the Irish revolutionary period was written by an outsider – especially if he was English – with no apparent axe to grind, gave the book a certain gravitas.

Much like Robert Kee's *Ireland – A History* written two decades later, *Ireland's Civil War* was written to give a non-Irish audience a balanced account of the Easter Rising, the War of Independence, the Treaty negotiations and the Civil War.

Step by step, Younger takes us through these events. He describes the atrocities committed on both sides but manages to inject some humour into the narrative. While on one side he discusses the futility of the summary executions, the reprisals and the tit-for-tat killings that took place, on the other hand he tells the story of Brigadier Gerard Lucas who was captured as a hostage by the IRA. Concerned to treat the captive, a keen angler, well, one of his jailers took him fishing, somewhat illegally, one night. When the General wondered the following day how come his fishing companion was so certain there'd be no trouble from the bailiffs, he was told that Seán, his nocturnal companion, *was* the chief bailiff.

An inherent strength of the book is its description of the political negotiations that took place between the English government and the Irish representatives leading up to the Treaty. Younger illustrates the pressures on both sides and gives the reader a deeper understanding of the crucial events that lead, almost inevitably, to the Civil War.

Sun Dancing

Geoffrey Moorhouse

On a holiday in the south-west of Ireland, Geoffrey Moorhouse, English author, climbed a headland in a day, as he called it, of 'newly rinsed clarity' and noticed for the first time two jagged shapes far out to sea. Later when he asked an old man about them, he was told that he had seen the Skelligs and that he would be forever restless until he set foot on them. The old man's prophecy proved to be correct. Although he had visited monasteries all over the world, nothing prepared him for the sense of peace he experienced on his first trip and which has been reinforced on every subsequent visit. Out of these visits the book *Sun Dancing*, published in 1997, was born.

The book is in two parts. The first section, entitled 'The Tradition', consists of seven short stories, one for each century, which capture the austere life of the monks who lived and prayed in that inhospitable rock over seven centuries. The second part, entitled 'The Evidence', is made up of approximately fifty short essays on the different references used during the first part, and enlarges on many aspects of the medieval monastic life glancingly mentioned there. Moorhouse himself thinks of the book as a novella with elaborate footnotes. It was nominated for the Booker Prize in 1997. He tells us that it:

> ...treats of the roots and essences of Irishness, including attitudes to penance and fasting which

now seem savage and even in the Middle Ages were thought to be exceptionally rigorous: of connections between medieval Ireland and places as remote as India, Central Asia, Egypt and Byzantium; of Irish peregrinations that left a lasting mark across the length and breath of continental Europe; of the early Desert Fathers and the effect that one of them had on the subsequent course of western art, of the Celtic genius for amalgamating pagan naturism with Christian theology, of the progression from a biblical understanding of creation to a scientific apprehension of the universe; of medieval sickness and poverty and violence, which have too often been coated in romantic humbug; of the isolated culture of Viking invasion, ecclesiastical Romanisation and Anglo-Norman settlement. Niall of the Nine Hostages, Cú Chulainn, Brian Ború, Patrick, Brendan, Columba and Brigid of Kildare cross these pages; as also do Paul of Thebes, Athanasios, Cassian, Anthony the Hermit, Origen, any number of popes, Olaf Tryggvason, Hieronymus Bosch and Gustave Flaubert.

In fact, and as promised by Moorhouse, *Sun Dancing* is a panorama of Early Christian Ireland and in all its vicissitudes, as lived by the monastic settlements which proliferated throughout the country. The prose is simple and clear and eminently accessible to the modern reader. There is a sense of joy and delight, as well as moments of wonderful peace and of deep spirituality throughout.

Hungry for Home

COLE MORETON

On 17 November 1953, a fishing boat called the *St Lawrence O'Toole* left Dingle harbour bound for the Blasket Islands. On board were two men from the Land Commission, Seán Goulding and Dan O'Brien, whose job it was to oversee the evacuation of the few remaining inhabitants of the Western Island. Although they did not succeed in achieving this fully, due to the inclement weather – only six islanders managed to leave – that journey opened the final chapter in the long history of Irish emigrations.

The number of emigrants in this case may have been small, involving only nine families, but the ramifications of their final departure were so extensive as to sound the death-knell of an indigenous native culture. In his fascinating book *Hungry For Home,* Cole Moreton explores what happened before, during and directly after this momentous event.

Born in London on 1967, and graduating from Middlesex University with a first-class honours degree in Contemporary Writing, Cole Moreton was to follow an extensive career as a journalist. He now lives in East Sussex with his wife and four children. *Hungry For Home*, first published in 2000, was his first book.

The story begins on Christmas Eve 1946. A horrific storm howls around the Blasket Islands. A man and his son are killing a sheep, a Christmas tradition on the island. When they return to their cottage Seáinín Ó Cearnaigh, the son, puts his hand to his

head and collapses. Because of the weather, the family is unable to seek medical help. Days later, the young man dies.

There is no consecrated ground in the island, so in order to give Seáinín a decent funeral, the body has to be brought to the mainland to be buried. After some days, the storm shows no sign of abating. Four men brave the raging seas and risk their lives in a fragile *naomhóg* so that the family can wake their dead son properly and their fellow islander can rest in peace.

Seáinín Ó Cearnaigh's death and funeral was the catalyst that finally resulted in the abandonment of the Blasket Islands. The islanders' struggle for survival had been heroic and, although their numbers were dwindling, they were enjoying a reasonable quality of life. It was, however, the isolation and the lack of political will to do anything about it that made the islanders realise that human habitation was no longer sustainable.

In an evenly-paced narrative, Moreton takes us through the story of the island's existence from its very first occupants right through to the final evacuation in 1953. It is the story of resilience and survival. It is the story of a unique way of life with all its traditions and eccentricities. It is the story of a particular Gaelic culture, its poetry and its folklore. Above all, it is a significant chapter in the story of the human race.

But the real value of *Hungry For Home* doesn't stop there. Moreton seeks out the survivors and follows their footsteps to new homes on the Dingle Peninsula and in Springfield, Massachusetts. In so doing he completes the journey and archives the complete story of that unique community.

District and Circle

Seamus Heaney

'There is an awful lot of it in it,' Seamus Heaney remarked ruefully as he looked at our Irish Poetry section. There certainly is and the nation is all the richer for it. The cliché of Ireland having a standing army of poets has outlived its original derogatory context. Now its soldiers are seen as craftsmen who fashion words so we can love and mourn. They sing our victories, bewail our losses and satirise our eccentricities. They are often the thin edge of revolution, the champions of individual freedom and political independence, the enemies of oppression. Poets are an essential component of the wellbeing of any nation and nowhere is this more evident than in Heaney's own collection, *District and Circle*.

Seamus Heaney was born in 1939 and brought up on a small farm called Mossbawn between the townlands of Toombridge and Castletown in County Derry. Educated at Anahorish Primary School, St Columb's in Derry and Queen's University in Belfast, he taught for a year in St Thomas's Intermediate School in Belfast where Michael McLaverty, the headmaster, encouraged his writing. He participated in the poetry circle organised by Philip Hobsbaum at Queen's University and was appointed lecturer in the English Department there in 1966. He published his first collection, *Death of a Naturalist*, in the same year.

Heaney's poetic landscape is both local and international. The heft of a spade in a potato field can inform his verse, as can the cosmic vision of Horace or Dante. This flexibility of vision allows

him to celebrate the routine daily tasks of honest endeavour as well as recognise the catastrophes – natural and man-made – that threaten to destroy the life of the individual. His verse is incredibly democratic, his use of words uncanny but above all his poetry has a warmth that is inviting, comforting and satisfying.

Poetry is essentially a personal experience and if the reader can find in a collection an image or thought that resounds, the poet has achieved his or her objective. When the poet can go beyond the personal and create an image that echoes through a community in a positive way, a country's need for its poets has been re-asserted. In *District and Circle*, there is a poem called 'Midnight Anvil' which begins:

> If I wasn't there
> When Barney Devlin hammered
> The midnight anvil
> I can still hear it: twelve blows
> Struck for the millennium.
> His nephew heard it
> In Edmunton, Alberta:
> The cellular phone
> Held high as a horse's ear
> Barney smiling to himself.

These lines beg the Utopian image of the whole world holding up its mobile phones to hear the twelve ringing blows of Barney Devlin's hammer as it strikes the midnight anvil, and for the space of these twelve blows at least, the world would be at ease with itself and at peace. To repeat the words of John Lennon:

> Imagine, just imagine.

List of Illustrations

Index of Authors

Index of Titles